HEROES VILLAINS

AND GHOSTS

FOLKLORE OF OLD CALIFORNIA

BY HECTOR LEE

CAPRA PRESS
1984

Cover and illustrations by Judy Sutcliffe
Design and typography by Cook/Sundstrom Associates

LIBRARY OF CONGRESS CATALOGING IN PUBLICATION DATA
Lee, Hector, 1908-
Heroes, villains, and ghosts.
Includes bibliographical references.
1. Legends—California.   I. Title
GR110.C3L44 1984   398′.352   84-7707
ISBN 0-88496-223-7 (pbk.)

Published by
CAPRA PRESS
P.O. Box 2068
Santa Barbara, Ca. 93120

HEROES, VILLAINS AND GHOSTS

CONTENTS

I. HEROES AND VILLAINS

He fought the deep forbidding snows, the bitter cold, and the rugged heights of the Sierra Nevadas to be for thirteen years the human link between California and the East.

Shanghaied into piracy, he became one of the first Americanos in California and founded a family dynasty where Pasadena is now.

Now a character of legend in Santa Cruz County, this remarkable stagecoach driver shared the dangers and adventures of life in the mining camps from Sonora to Placerville.

General Mariano Vallejo may have been wise, but he was no match for the wily Frenchman whose con game taught him a lesson about sugar.

She met her fate at the Jersey Bridge in Downieville, and became a "first" in California history, but whether she was guilty remains a moot question.

Even if a ruthless criminal could outlive his bloodstained past and become a model citizen, old Temelec mansion could not keep its secret.

He is honored in place names and remembered in history, but the circumstances of his death are a mystery.

III. BEHIND THE SCENES

FOREWORD

A legend is a story told by a lot of people. It is about real or presumably real persons, places, or events, and it survives in the memory of the folk because it serves one or more cultural or psychological needs. It may glorify a hero or villain, explain some geographical feature, memorialize an event, or provide a context for wishful thinking. And sometimes, like a ghost story which is a local legend, its function may be primarily to entertain.

Legends stay alive because they are worthy of being retold, and every storyteller has the right to tell them in his own way. That is why, in their survival, legends tend to drift away from the actual facts in order to convey an "essential truth" which may be more interesting than the historical truth. In his own version of a story, therefore, every storyteller retains what he considers the most important facts, leaves out what he thinks is less relevant, and adds what he deems necessary to make the story better.

All the legends in this book have their roots in California history or have emerged from the memory of some real person. However, they cannot be called real folklore, strictly speaking, because they are not here copied from the exact words of "folk" informants. I have exercised the storyteller's privilege of retelling them in my own way. In that sense, perhaps, I am one of the folk.

I have chosen these legends because I think they express a vital part of the mystique of California. In an earlier book, Tales of California, *I told some of the region's best legends—stories about Sam Brannan, the outlaws Sontag and Evans, Lotta Crabtree, Lola Montez, Ishi, and others; consequently, they are not included here, but I think this volume is equally representative of the scope and variety of California legendry. And since many teachers found the first collection useful as a text, I have added brief notes "Behind the Scenes" for those who wish to pursue some legends further in terms of historical, traditional, or narrative background.*

Hector H. Lee
Sonoma State University
Rohnert Park, California

I. HEROES AND VILLAINS

Snowshoe Thompson

It was late in the fall of 1855, and Sacramento had hunched its shoulders against the first autumn rain. This would mean snow in the mountains and mud in the streets of the valley towns below, but it was welcome after the long dry summer. Along the boardwalks in downtown Sacramento the people walked fast, leaning into the wind-driven rain, or ducked into doorways to stand a few minutes before scurrying on.

But one man seemed not to be in a hurry. Tall, raw-boned, muscular, and obviously toughened by exposure to the elements, he strode rather than walked, as if to defy the spray in his face and ignore the rivulets that ran down from his drooping wide-brimmed hat and over the shoulders of his long coat.

He passed the wide door of the hotel, then paused and looked in the window. The lobby was empty except for one man lounging in a big leather chair, smoking a cigar, and contentedly watching the scene outside. He studied the seated man for a moment, hesitating, and then turned and entered the lobby. Some newspapers were lying in the chair beside the man with the cigar, and the newcomer picked them up and sat down.

Cigar said nothing, and the big man began to fumble through

the papers. After a long silence, Cigar began to feel embarrassed by such unacknowledged human proximity and decided it was time to open a conversation.

"You new here?"

"Yes."

"Been up in the diggings, have you?" Cigar noted that the man was young, younger than he seemed at first glance, and stalwart young men always went to the gold fields.

"Oh, yes. I came here to look for gold, but I didn't find any," answered the stranger in an unmistakable Scandinavian accent. Then as if for an afterthought he added, "Also I been to try ranching a little, too, but that ain't no good either. Now I t'ink maybe I find me a steady job from the paper here."

"Where you come from?" asked Cigar.

"I begin from Norway, but I been here some time now. My name is John Thompson."

"Pleased to meet ya," grunted the Cigar. "So you're out of work."

"Maybe I'll find somet'ing," Thompson said. "I just see by the paper here that a feller by the name Chopening wants somebody to carry the mail for him."

"Yeah, I heard about that. Old man Chopening wants to weasel out on his contract to carry the mail. Supposed to run from Sacramento to Salt Lake, there and back. I guess he done all right in the summer, but he couldn't make it through the mountains in winter. Nobody can; the snow's too deep."

The Cigar was right about that. A man named Chopening had indeed taken the mail contract. It was easy to carry the mail over the Sierra Nevada mountains in summer by mule pack, but in winter he found it a different matter. His partners had been killed by the Indians, he had lost his horses and mules in the blizzards, and now he couldn't find anyone to do the hard and dangerous job for him. The mail could move from Sacramento to Placerville, the last outpost town in the foothills, but there it stopped. The mountain passes were already snowbound.

Chopening needed a man who understood the mountains, who

was at home in the snow, and who could handle himself on skis.

"I t'ink maybe I'd like to try that," said Thompson.

The Cigar looked him over. "How old are you?"

"I'm twenty-eight."

"Well, you're a prime specimen, I must say. You just might make it if you don't get shot by Indians or lost in the snow or froze by a blizzard or get et up by the wolves. Tell you what I'd do: I'd go up to Placerville and talk to the postmaster about it. He might put you on for a trial run, anyway."

When Thompson left the hotel his mind was made up. He had had some experience with skis in Norway, and he wanted to be busy. The next day he was on the stage to Placerville, and three days later he presented himself to the postmaster. With him he carried a pair of skis which he had carved himself out of sturdy smooth-grained oak poles. But they were not just ordinary skis. They were about ten feet long, and the two of them weighed twenty-five pounds. No one had ever seen such big skis before. But even more unusual was that the curves in front were not only higher and wider than normal, they also had delicately carved decorations on the tips. At that time skis were called snowshoes, and although ordinary snowshoes were in common use by trappers and Indians throughout the Sierra, this strange gear that Thompson had was unique.

The postmaster explained that he could not give him a job. Chopening had the mail contract, and he was nowhere to be found. He had probably gone back to Salt Lake City and abandoned the contract.

The next day Thompson came back. The answer was the same. On the third day when the postmaster opened up, there was Thompson and his long skis, waiting. The mail was piling up, and something had to be done. The postmaster was growing desperate.

"Look here," he said. "Contract or no contract, if we could get this mail over the mountains to Genoa, that's in Nevada in the Utah Territory not far from Carson City, it could go on from there by regular stage. I don't have the authority to give you the mail, but if you want to chance it I guess I can. I can't promise you any money, though; you better understand that right off."

"I t'ink maybe I'd like to try that," said Thompson. He didn't know that he was embarking on an enterprise that would last more than thirteen years.

As soon as he got the job he established a regular schedule. He left Placerville every two weeks on the dot, rain or shine, ice or snow. The distance was about ninety miles. He more or less followed the old Carson Trail that passed south of Lake Tahoe, but he gradually worked out short-cuts that made the route a little easier.

It would take him three days to make the trip from Placerville eastward over the mountains. Because of the long slopes on the western side of the Sierra he had more climbing distance going up, but when he reached the top he could come down very rapidly on the other side. It took him only two days to make the return trip from Genoa. He carried no blankets because such impediments would only slow him down. For food he took only a few biscuits and some beef or venison jerky.

In summer the trip was very pleasant, but he was not needed so much then. Others could carry the mail when travel was easy, but in winter he was back on the job. If he got cold he would crawl into a cave somewhere, or if he wanted to sleep he would try to find an old stump, set it afire, and lie in the snow near it until he was ready to move on. Such an expedient was none too comfortable, however, for he had to keep turning like meat on a spit to avoid roasting on one side while freezing on the other.

The usual load strapped to his back was sixty to ninety pounds of mail. Included in this load might also be the lighter necessities of life such as medicines for the people of Genoa, who paid him a little for the favor. He even carried a printing press over—not all at once, of course, but one piece at a time. It was assembled in Genoa and used there for many years. Normally, freight would come from the west—San Francisco and Sacramento—to be delivered in summer, but the light mail would come from both directions. On the route from Salt Lake westward, Genoa was the last outpost before the high mountain barrier, and from 1855 to 1868 during the winter months Snowshoe Thompson was the only living link between the east and west coasts in this part of California.

To a man of his stamina the trip was actually exhilarating. Gliding down the long snow-added ridges, with the cold wind stinging his face, reminded him of his youth in Norway. Leaning from side to side as he swept around the curves, or sailing with increasing speed down the long slopes to dip and then rise up the hills beyond and go sailing in a graceful arc down again, gave him the feeling that a big bird must have, free to swoop and rise again at will. And there was always joy in the sensation of keeping his head and the load on his shoulders floating smoothly against the ever-changing beat of the terrain under his feet, especially when the snow was crusted and rough, with his knees and back responding to each jolt like some perfectly tuned machine under full control.

When there was no snow or the pack was too thin for skiing, Thompson trudged on foot and there was for him a sensation of great power in the exercise. Especially on those cold, still nights when the granulated snow was frozen dry he would listen to the squeaking sound his boots made as they crunched in regular rhythm along the trail. And each year he watched the spring unfold, when the granite crags began to rise out of the receding layers of white, and at unexpected intervals the heavy frosting on the fir trees would break loose and fall and the drooping limbs released of their winter burden would spring back to normal symmetry ready for the new season of life.

At first he carried a revolver with him for protection, but then he found that if he left the gun behind he could carry an extra packet of letters; so he went without it. On one occasion, however, he regretted the rashness of such economy. He was going up the trail high in the mountains, and he heard a pack of wolves ahead of him. As he came up over a ridge he saw them; they had killed some small animal and were snarling, yapping, and fighting over the carcass. Obviously they were hungry; they growled and snapped at each other as if ready to kill. Thompson saw, too, that they were big. If they attacked him there would be no defense against them. He did not slow down, however, but continued to move steadily toward them. He remembered from some folklore in Norway that you must never run away from wolves; if you do they will sense your fear and tear you to pieces. So he kept coming toward them.

The wolves saw him and stopped fighting over their small carcass. They watched him. He came on toward them. The leader of the pack crouched low and slowly moved near the trail that Thompson was to pass. He kept on coming. The wolf sat down and snarled and showed his fangs. Suddenly he let out a terrific howl, and all the other wolves moved in close and formed a half-circle around him beside the trail. But Snowshoe Thompson came steadily toward them. As he came close they snarled and showed their teeth and crouched. He did not slow down or turn aside; he came near them, and passed them, and went on up the trail and over the hill beyond. The wolves watched him go. Then they returned to their unfinished meal and lost interest in the man who had walked among them.

On another occasion Snowshoe Thompson was picking his way through the snowdrifts in the pass south of Lake Tahoe. He knew of a small abandoned cabin nearby and decided to stop there for an hour or so and get warm. He was tired, the cold wind cut through to the bone, and his whiskers were glazed into a coarse white mask. He found the cabin, approached the door, and leaned his skis against the snow-piled roof. Before entering, he paused to listen. There was something inside, something that made a sound like a faint groan. He entered cautiously, thinking it might be some wild animal.

Inside he found a man lying on the floor. The room was cold. The man had burned all the wood and even the furniture, what little there had been, but the fire had finally gone out. The man was only half conscious, and his words came hard. Both his feet had

"But Snowshoe Thompson came steadily toward them."

been frozen, and they were swollen and gangrenous. Thompson knew the man would perish if left there very long, but there was no way to get him out.

He found some wood outside and built another fire. He gave the man some food and made him as comfortable as possible. In an interval of consciousness the man told him his name was James Sisson, but there was little more to be learned from him. Thompson knew that help must be obtained quickly, so without delay he closed the cabin door and hastened on to Genoa.

It didn't take long to muster a rescue party. Fortified with brandy, food and blankets, and dragging a large sled, they set out immediately with Thompson leading to show the way. Sisson was still alive when they reached the cabin. With deliberate haste they gave him food and stimulant, wrapped him in blankets, tied him to the sled, and headed back to civilization.

A doctor who had been called from Carson was waiting when they reached Genoa. It was near midnight when they lifted the stricken man from the sled and put him on a table. Lamps and lanterns were held close, and the doctor began his examination. Every man in the room knew the seriousness of the situation, for each in his own way had faced and conquered this common mortal enemy, the sub-zero blasts of the terrible Sierra Nevadas.

The doctor shook his head gravely. "Both legs have been froze quite awhile," he said. The men nodded; they expected as much. "The gangrene is just starting, but it can't be stopped," he went on. "Both feet will have to come off."

"Well, Doc, go ahead and take 'em off," said the men.

The doctor shook his head. "Can't do that. At least, not without chloroform. His heart's too weak; he'd die on us right here if he didn't have chloroform."

"Well?"

"Well, there isn't any. Not in Carson, and not in Virginia City. I happen to know that for a fact. My guess is that the closest chloroform would be maybe in Placerville, more likely in Sacramento."

The men looked at each other again, but no face among them showed anything but despair in this new complication. Finally, Snowshoe Thompson, who had been sitting on the floor near the stove, got to his feet.

"I guess I could go for some," he said.

The incredulous faces turned to him. "You crazy, man? You just come about ninety miles over from Placerville, and then back up to that cabin and back. You may be strong as a mule, but no man's all that good."

"I t'ink maybe I'd like to try," Thompson said simply.

So he set out immediately, back up the long trail over the snowbound mountain the long ninety miles to Placerville. There was no chloroform there, so he went on another forty miles to Sacramento. He got what he needed and without delay began the hard, cold journey back to Genoa. He reached there in time for Sisson to have his operation. The legs were lost, but the life was saved.

Thompson settled in Nevada. He had owned a small ranch west of Sacramento, but he sold that and bought a ranch in Diamond Valley near Genoa, which he worked in the summer when he was not carrying the mail. In his spare time he taught many young men to ski and thus promoted an interest in skiing in the Sierra. Occasionally he would participate in skiing events himself.

A skiing club was organized in northern California, and on one occasion when they were meeting at La Porte, northeast of Oroville, Thompson came to compete with them. He was recognized as a formidable jumper—not graceful, but daring. Long before records had been set and recorded in ski jumping, he was said to have jumped over a hundred feet in rough mountain terrain. If true, that would have been a spectacular jump at any time.

When the Chinese laborers cut the railroad through from California eastward in 1868 there was no more need for Snowshoe Thompson to carry the mails. But in spite of his faithful service he was never paid for these thirteen years of strenuous mountain skiing. He had supported himself by the meager yield of his ranch in summer, and in winter of course he could not work because he was carrying the mail. But no contract had ever been made, and without a contract the government could not pay him. The owner of the mail contract had defaulted, and nobody knew who would pay him.

From time to time the miners and other citizens of Genoa would take up a collection, and it is said that with this help he paid for his ranch. No one knows for sure, but the miners and frontiersmen had good reason to show their appreciation in this tangible form. But according to the records, for his work of thirteen years carrying the mail, he collected only $80.22.

In 1872 he decided to go back to Washington to see if Congress would help him. He took a petition signed by a thousand citizens in support of his claim. He was asking for $6,000 as back salary for services rendered. But this time he traveled by train.

But before he could reach Washington he once more had to face a contest with the elements. In Wyoming, about twenty-five miles from Laramie, a storm caught them and the train was snowbound. Considering the delay harder to endure than the snow, Thompson decided to walk the twenty-five miles into Laramie. A chance acquaintance on the train asked to go along, and the two set out on foot.

The partner, however, soon grew tired and gave up; so Thompson had to help him the last few miles. In Laramie he found that there was no way out. The trains east of there were also snowed in. The first movable train was in Cheyenne, and that was about fifty miles further on. So once again Thompson set out on foot, caught the train in Cheyenne, and proceeded on to Washington.

Of course, by the time he reached Washington he was a highly publicized and famous figure. The newspapers played him up as the only man who had been able to get through from the West Coast. This brought him both attention and sympathy. Everyone said his cause was just, and an enthusiastic public wished him well.

But neither Congress nor the Post Office Department granted him any money. So he gave up and came home penniless to his acres in Diamond Valley. In 1876 he caught pneumonia, and that, together with a liver ailment, caused his death.

In 1945 there was organized a Snowshoe Thompson Memorial Ski Meet, and his name is remembered in legend. An inspired eulogist might have praised him as a great man who served so many for so long and so well. It might have been said that he did not do it for gain; he certainly made no money. Nor did he do it for glory or honor, except the honor that comes from the respect of his fellow men; he got full measure of that. He was a gentle giant who saw a job that needed to be done, and he did it. All this might have been said. But it wasn't.

Today in Genoa his grave is marked by a lonely old tombstone. Carved on it, along with his name, are two crossed skis.

Joseph Chapman, El Inglés

WHEN JOE CHAPMAN awoke he realized that he was on board a ship. It was dark, and his head ached. He heard the squeak and strain of the rigging and felt the rocking of the ship, and when he looked aloft he saw that the vessel was under full sail. As his head cleared he began to realize what had happened to him. The last he remembered was walking past a dark alley in Boston, and now here. He had been shanghaied. The sails above him were full, and he knew that he was well out to sea.

His next realization was of several pairs of legs and feet standing on the deck beside him. When his eyes focused he saw several men looming over him, and in the half darkness they seemed to be grinning.

"Time to wake up, lad; you're a sailor now." The voice was not unkind, but more mocking than gentle. He sensed peril and said nothing.

"Take him below," ordered the voice. "Tomorrow we'll find out whether we've caught a marlin or a herring." It was obviously a mate speaking, and Joe sensed that here was authority not to be trifled with. He went below without protest. Besides, his head hurt.

The next morning he was put to work. Fortunately he knew a little about ships. He was—or to be more exact under the present circumstances, he had been—an apprentice to a shipbuilder in Boston. This was no small asset, which he promptly made known to his fellows, some of whom had been taken aboard like himself without their full knowledge or consent. He knew that in time his skills would serve him well, and they did; it was not long before he became the ship's carpenter.

As the days went by, he assimilated all the knowable facts of his situation. The ship was a freebooter with no fixed destination except where the captain chose to exercise his talents in the pirate's trade. Even at this late date, 1817, such entrepreneurs were not uncommon, and the captain, one Hipolyte Bouchard, prided himself on his finesse and gentility as well as his daring. His home base was Buenos Aires, where several privateers—survivors of a more hectic past—found periodic haven, but he carried no flag except as needed in a friendly port. The crew were of many nationalities.

Joe decided to make the best of a bad situation and became friendly with a few of his fellows. One in particular, a Negro who called himself Tom Fisher, became his closest friend with whom he could share his confidential thoughts. Fisher, a runaway slave, could listen and keep his mouth shut.

Joe's home ties were not too binding, so he was able to accept this new adventure with good spirit. What else could he do? Obviously Fate was at the helm. He remembered a quotation that had been passed on to him by his uncle, who made pretentions at being a literary man: "There is a tide in the affairs of men which, taken at the flood, leads on to fortune." A tide had swept him up, and he might as well ride it as far as it would take him. Perhaps, after all, this was to be his fortune

The tides in question, and good winds, took them south around Cape Horn and then in a wide sweep northward. They touched at various tropical islands, but found nothing in particular worth taking, and eventually they reached the Sandwich Islands, where they stayed several months. Here Captain Bouchard recruited enough Kanaka sailors to fill out his crew. Life on the islands was pleasant enough, but profits were slim, and the men were growing restless. The tides had not as yet led them to any great fortune.

Eventually they pulled anchor and the ship headed eastward, straight toward the coast of America; and in November, 1818, she entered Monterey harbor. Here at last would be booty worth taking. Captain Bouchard sent a note to the commandante of the presidio demanding that he surrender the town or suffer the consequences. If he failed to surrender, the town would be destroyed. While the pirates waited for an answer, Joe and Tom Fisher looked to their cutlasses and with the other men made ready for the assault.

After some delay, Governor Sola sent a note refusing to surrender. Then he ordered his gunners at the fort to open fire on the ship. Their shots missed. Bouchard had several howitzers on his deck, and he had his men fire on the town. A few shots crashed into buildings, causing some damage and much panic among the Mexicans there. Joe and Tom were among the landing party that went ashore ready for a fight.

"I didn't ask to be here," he remarked to Tom Fisher, "but now that I am, I might as well make the best of it. We might even get rich out of this."

"Maybe yes, maybe no," was the only answer he got. Tom was willing to steal from any whites, Spanish or otherwise, but he was not so sure he wanted to kill anybody.

Fortunately for all concerned, Governor Sola had had time to evacuate the town. Most of the families, taking what they could carry, had scampered inland to the Rancho del Rey, the present site of Salinas, leaving the town to the pirates.

The looting was easy. Whatever valuables they could find were confiscated in the name of free enterprise—a little jewelry, some silverware but not much gold, and in the larger dwellings a goodly supply of very fancy clothing. The valuables were dumped into sacks and carried back to the ship. The clothing was of no particular value to the pirates, but provided much pleasure for the Kanaka sailors, who decked themselves out in boots, serapes, sombreros, and richly colored skirts. For Joe Chapman the tide of success was rising. He had enjoyed the exhilaration of victory and had acquired for his share a little booty of some value. This was more property than he had ever possessed before, and he had not had to kill anybody to get it. When the ship sailed out of Monterey harbor Joseph Chapman the poor apprentice from Boston was a professional pirate.

A week later the buccaneers put in at a cove near Santa Barbara. The hacienda and outbuildings of the Rancho Refugio could be seen on the headland above the cove, and the place looked prosperous. There would be gold, silver, and jewelry here, and it would be easier to strike such a place than to risk a military encounter with the soldiers stationed in Santa Barbara. At dusk several boats were lowered, and the landing party slid down the ropes and took their positions at the oars. This would be easier than Monterey. They beached their boats, scrambled up the trail-worn cliff, and ran across the broad tableland to attack the defenseless rancho, hungry for plunder.

What the pirates did not know was that riders from Monterey had brought the news, and a strange ship entering the cove near Santa Barbara was not a surprise. Reinforcements to the garrison had been sent up from Los Angeles. And even more to the point, the big, prosperous, fully manned Rancho Refugio was owned by the Ortega family. Spanish California had its aristocrisy, and the Ortegas were part of it. They were wealthy and powerful, their cattle ranged over thousands of acres, their vaqueros were skilled riders and knew their craft, and no one entered their domain without permission.

The looting started. The pirates raced through the gates to the big hacienda and burst open the heavy oak doors. Women screamed, children ran, and a few shots were fired from behind walls and through the grilled windows. Joe Chapman had a pistol in his waistband, but he didn't need it; the cutlass that he brandished was terrifying enough. This would be easy.

Suddenly heavier gunfire was heard in the patio. Soldiers had

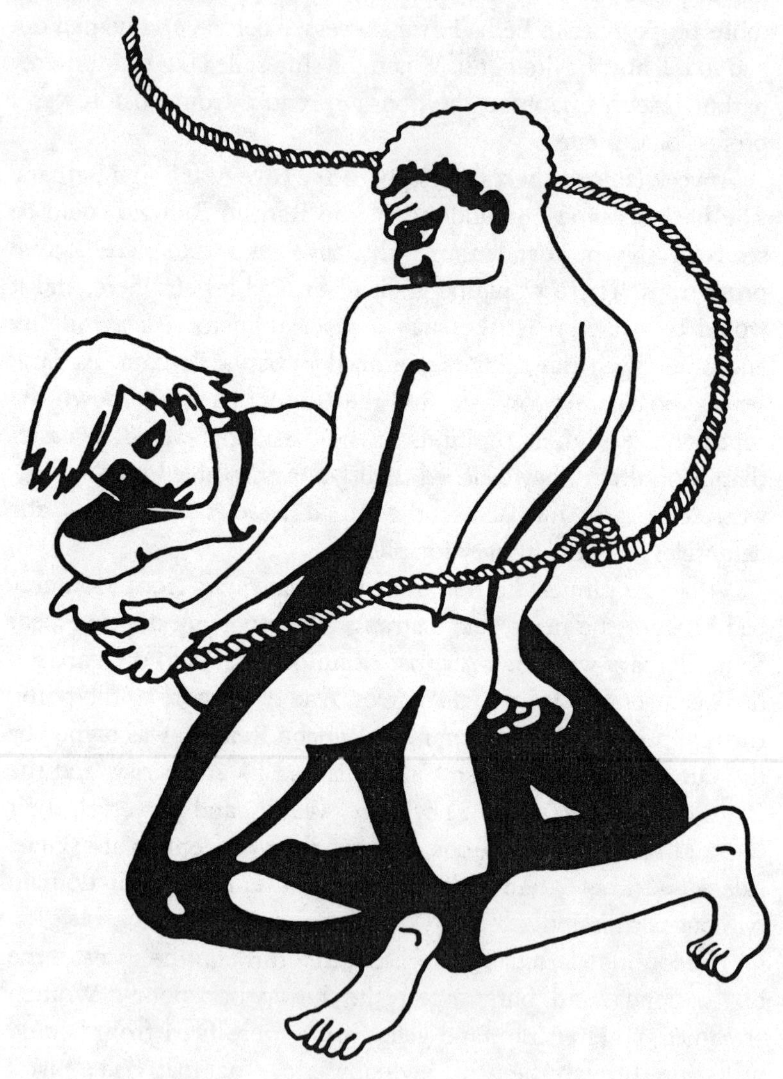

"Surrounded by menacing cowboys..."

arrived from the garrison at Santa Barbara, and to their surprise the pirates were outnumbered. The tide of battle quickly turned, and the attackers found themselves on the defensive. Sacking the Ortega rancho was not such a good idea after all, and the sensible thing to do was withdraw as fast as possible. They scampered in confusion toward their boats on the beach, intent only on getting out of range of the soldiers, who were still firing on them.

All at once a new peril swooped in upon them. The Ortega vaqueros materialized from nowhere and were riding furiously toward them. The pirates tumbled down the steep cliff and raced for their waiting boats, but the riders did not stop for the cliffs; their sure-footed Mexican ponies plunged over the rim and slid to the beach, closing in on the terrified pirate rout.

Joe slipped on a loose rock and lost his footing. He fell sideways and literally rolled down to the beach below. Already his companions were tumbling into the boats and grabbing the oars. Clearly, he was to be left behind. But seeing the situation, one of his comrades ran back from the boat to help him to his feet, and together they waded into the water. It was his friend, Tom Fisher.

The other pirates were in the boats now and were pulling out to deep surf. Tom and Joe might have made it, but the horsemen were upon them swinging their riatas over their heads. Both Tom and Joe were lassoed and dragged gasping to the shore like wild steers. By now the other pirates in the boats were well out of reach and pulling for the waiting ship as fast as they could, and these two were prisoners.

They were dragged back up the cliff to the shelf of level ground and were allowed to stand up, surrounded by menacing Mexican cowboys armed with ropes and knives. They might have been killed immediately, but their strange appearance turned the anger of the Mexicans to wonder. Never had they seen a young man with such fair skin, long yellow hair, and blue eyes; nor had they ever seen a Negro. There was much jabbering in Spanish while their fate was being decided.

Suddenly the tide changed again. Another person had joined the group. It was a girl on a beautiful black horse. She studied them for a moment or two and then gave a command which was instantly obeyed. Apparently, they were not to be killed after all, at least not yet. Instead, they were taken, this time with less violence, back to the hacienda. They were prisoners, but the girl had saved their lives and that was something. She watched with obvious interest as their hands were tied and they were delivered to the soldiers from the garrison.

"Shanghaied again," Joe thought to himself. His tide had turned, and once again he began to speculate on how to make the best of a bad situation. He and Tom were taken to Santa Barbara and delivered to the commandante of the presidio, who ordered them to be locked up until he could decide what to do with them.

Later that night Captain Bouchard sent another party of desperadoes ashore to burn the little village near the ranch and look for his missing men, but they could not be found nor could the raiders find any booty of value. There was little satisfaction in their reprisal, and the next morning the pirate ship sailed away. Two weeks later it appeared off the coast of San Juan Capistrano where the pirates sacked the mission. Then Captain Bouchard and his buccaneers sailed away and were never heard of again on the California coast.

In Santa Barbara the fate of Joseph Chapman and Tom Fisher was still uncertain. They could not understand Spanish, and no one at the presidio could understand them; here was a problem that obviously had to be decided at a higher level. Meanwhile, the invaders were kept under guard and the announcement was made that if anyone wanted them and would be responsible for producing them upon demand in case of a formal hearing—well, he could have them.

Corporal Antonio Maria Lugo was interested. He had come up from Los Angeles as part of the reinforcements sent in haste when word of the danger from pirates was brought, and would be returning in a few days. These strange creatures from outer space might be of use to him as servants if they could ever learn to understand his orders. If not—the Devil take them!

It was evening when Lugo and his little squad of cavalry rode up to his door near the plaza in Los Angeles. When his wife went into the yard to greet him she saw a strange sight, indeed. On the horse behind Lugo and still clinging to him was the wretched sailor.

"What is it you have there, old man?"

"I don't know for certain, but one thing is sure, it can't ride a horse. I was afraid the fellow would fall off, so I had to bring him this way. He is a prisoner that we must keep—for whatever worth he may be to us."

"Is he a Christian?"

"That I don't know, either. I can't understand him. I think he says he speaks English. This man is on parole to me, so we must make him comfortable and feed him; then tomorrow we shall find out what he can do. There was another one we captured, a Negro, but he is still in Santa Barbara. This one we'll have to call *El Inglés.*"

And so *El Inglés*, the Englishman, became part of the Lugo household. To make the best of an uncertain situation, he set about immediately to learn Spanish. It just might be that here was another tide that would carry him back to fame and fortune if he could handle himself well.

He was an eager learner. His mastery of Spanish was admirable, and he quickly made himself valuable to the Lugos and other families in the village. As the months went by he grew in importance, and the respect of the community for him grew. Not all the services he rendered can be known, but in legend it was told that when he noticed the Mexican women tediously pounding and grinding corn into meal on stone *metates*, he devised and built for them a grist mill and the toil of the women was reduced and they were grateful.

It was told that construction on the little church which was being built across from the plaza had slowed to a halt because the heavy timbers needed for rafters could not be found; so Chapman talked Lugo into giving him a crew of Indians to get the job done. He and his Indians, with tools for cutting and hewing, and with *carretas* for hauling, went to the mountains and brought back the necessary timbers. Thus the church could be finished, now under Chapman's supervision, and Father Sanchez was grateful. The job was so well done that when the earthquakes came this church stood fast; its roof and walls were held in place by good timber.

It was told that Chapman helped to improve the economy of Los Angeles by building a boat with which otters could be hunted off the coast. He constructed the boat in Los Angeles, and with the help of his Indians moved it in sections to San Pedro where it was assembled and launched. It proved quite seaworthy, and from then on Los Angeles could take good furs for as long as the otters lasted.

It was told that he could heal the sick and repair the wounded. But it was his skill with tools and his ability to solve the engineering problems of construction that gave him distinction and won for him the friendship and appreciation of the Mexicans. He was no longer called *El Inglés*, the Englishman; now he was Señor José Chapman.

"You know, you are still my prisoner," Lugo reminded him one day. "I am still responsible for what you do, but I have a plan. Father Sanchez tells me that if you would be baptized into the Catholic Church, and if you would become a Mexican citizen—the process is not so difficult—then I think you would be excused for the affair at the Ortega Rancho."

He readily agreed to the terms, and within a year he was officially Señor José Chapman, a Catholic and a Mexican with his freedom and a full pardon. Once again he was riding a good tide.

By this time Lugo was ready to have another idea. He and his wife had been whispering about it for a long time and had come to a decision. "It is now necessary," Lugo began with great seriousness one day, "that you should have a wife." At Chapman's look of surprise, a broad grin spread across Lugo's face.

Into Joe's mind flashed the thought, "Well! I am about to be shanghaied again!" But his old dream of wealth and influence began once again to rise in his mind. All he said was, "Well, you may be right."

It was not long before the stars moved into a most favorable position and an opportunity came. Something had gone wrong in a construction project at the Mission Santa Ynez north of Santa Barbara, and the priests there had sent an urgent request to Father Sanchez. Could he lend them the American wonder-worker to help repair the building? Señor Lugo and his señora immediately saw far beyond the simple matter of Santa Ynez Mission.

"You will go first to Santa Barbara and then to Santa Ynez, and I must go with you. I can arrange things. You will meet the Señorita Guadalupe Ortega there. She is very beautiful and much woman—but you already know that."

"How should I know that?"

"Ah, but you have met her. She is the one who saved your life when the vaqueros were about to kill you at Refugio. You can be sure she looked at you that night. And her father is very rich. You think about it, but don't take too long."

The next day they started for Santa Barbara. A fiesta was arranged, and the two young people met, this time under the most favorable of circumstances. The young lady was indeed beautiful, and her father, who was very rich, seemed to like the tall American with yellow hair and a talent for building things. Señor Lugo was on the job, and before long a time was set for the wedding. The girl, of course, could have said no, but according to the legend no such thought entered her mind.

So after the proper interval, during which time Chapman was busy at Santa Ynez, the happy ceremonies took place. The wedding lasted three days, and Señorita Guadalupe Ortega became Señora José Chapman. Together and in great splendor they rode back to Los Angeles, and with them went an old friend, Tom Fisher.

Two years later the Chapmans bought a large ranch near what is now Pasadena, and their friend Fisher became one of their vaqueros riding with the Indians and Mexicans to round up the

cattle for their hides and tallow. It is told in the legend that the
Chapmans lived happily ever after. They had several children, who
also married well and prospered, and their descendants now bear
distinguished names in California history.

Later, when the first American adventurers found their way to
California as trappers, mariners, or explorers, they reported seeing
the wealthy American-Mexican at the San Gabriel Mission tinker-
ing with his gadgets and making wooden toys for the children.
This was how Jedediah Smith met him in 1825, and this was how
he lived out his happy life.

In 1849, Tom Fisher left the ranch and drifted out to the gold
fields to seek his fortune in a new adventure and was never heard
from again. In that same year Joe Chapman, José el Inglés, died.
But he still lives in legend as California's first American.

Charley Parkhurst

CHARLEY PARKHURST was dying. The old fellow lay unattended on his crude wooden bed in the little cabin where he had spent his latter days as a recluse. The people of Watsonville were vaguely aware of him as a queer sort of duck who preferred to live alone, and few knew or cared that before making this final stop Charley Parkhurst had been one of the two or three most famous stagecoach drivers in the West.

His one known friend, George Harmon, came down from Soquel once in a while just to see how he was getting along, but his repeated offers of help were always refused. When the aging hermit grew too sick to get about and Harmon realized that he couldn't last much longer, he said again what he had often said before: "Charley, I think you'd better let me call in the doctor; he might be able to help you."

"Hell, no," snorted Charley. "Ain't no doctor goin' to come poking around in me. I know I'm a goner, so let it be. Dyin' is a one-way ticket for a ride you have to take alone. Any damn doctor comes nosin' around here, I'll blow his head off."

And that was that. Charley died alone, and the shrunken old body was discovered when Harmon came along a day or two later. The date of death was officially noted at December 28, 1879.

Not much was ever found out about Charley's early years. It was said that he had been born in New Hampshire in 1812 and as a child had worked with his uncle on a farm; but the work was dull, the uncle was strict, and the lad had a mind of his own. He ran away from home. In Providence, Rhode Island, he got a job as a stable boy and coachman for a Mr. Childs and later a man named Ebenezer Bach, who taught him to manage horses and care for them and love them. Eventually he went to Georgia where he became a stage driver, and when his employer, Jim Birch, came west to operate a stage line known as the California Stage Company, Charley came along. "I aim to be the best damn driver in California," he said, and he meant it.

The first run was between Oakland and San Jose. Here driving was simple. The ground was level, the roads were good, and four horses could easily pull the coach at a fast clip. But during the Gold Rush of the 1850s and '60s the Mother Lode country was calling, and Charley responded. In middle age now Charley had both the experience needed and the daring that comes only with the utmost self-confidence. From Stockton to Mariposa and from Sacramento to Placerville the roads were rough, the hills steep, the dugway passages narrow with sharp curves, and the constant danger of rolling boulders or washouts always lurked unexpectedly ahead.

On such roads it took a team of six horses to bring the swaying, bucking, sometimes top-heavy coach up through the mountains. Coming downhill over such roads called for the utmost strength at the brakes, judgment in matching speed to terrain, and skill in keeping the leaders their distance ahead of the swing team. Good drivers were scarce, the pay was good, and a kind of aristocracy emerged among them. Charley gained the recognition he wanted as one of the best.

On the Wells Fargo mail and express routes the drivers had to maintain a strict schedule. A driver was disgraced if he brought his coach into a station more than half an hour late without a very good reason. Every ten or twelve miles, depending on the geography, a swing station was maintained where the passengers could rest and get refreshments for fifteen or twenty minutes while the hostlers changed teams.

The romantic picture of the Concord coach with six matched horses all white or black, charging along the curving road at breakneck speed was not always borne out by the facts. Most drivers, of course, liked to come into a station or through a town at full speed for dramatic effect. The horses quickly learned this game, knowing full well that once out of town they could settle back to a reasonable gait for the long stretch between stations.

In physical appearance, Parkhurst was strong and stocky, about five and a half feet tall. His barrel-chested upper figure and broad bottom, with small hands and short legs, gave him an ant-like configuration, and like that worthy creature his sting was sharp. Once a smart-aleck driver, trying to be clever, said, "Charley, it's four o'clock and time for you to get that heavy beam of yours up into the dickey seat."

Charley snapped back, "You'd be broad in the beam, too, if you'd drove as many miles as I have. Ain't no snakey slither-hips like you ever goin' to outlast me on a tough run, so you can just put that in your pipe and smoke it and keep your compliments to yourself." The joker accepted the rebuke, and that ended the raillery.

Although Charley could get as dirty as the next one around the corral or when the roads were mud up to the axle, he took pride in neatness and style when he appeared in the saloon, the boarding house, or the station ready for departure. His gloves were made of the finest buckskin that the Indians could fashion to his order, with wide gauntlets decorated with beads, embroidery, or colored silk ornaments. His hats were of felt with a low crown, medium brim, and a fancy band of snakeskin or leather studded with silver. He wore a handkerchief about the neck, as did all the drivers, for protection against the dust in

summer and the friction of the coat collar in winter. His feet
were small, but his custom-made boots had three-inch heels that
compensated for his lack of height. His face was dark brown,
leathery and tough, but whether this swarthiness was due to
some racial mixture or merely the prolonged exposure to weather,
no one knew or cared to guess.

Up and down the Sierra and throughout the Big Valley all the
drivers knew each other. Their bonds of fellowship forged by
the work itself were constantly reinforced by their mutual social
life at the stations that marked division points along their
routes or in major towns where normal runs would begin and
end, such as Sacramento, Hangtown-turned-Placerville, Jackson,
Sonora, Mariposa, Merced. At favorite saloons in such places
this fraternity, sometimes called Knights of the Whip, would
assemble at night to drink beer or harder stuff, smoke cigars,
and talk over their adventures on the road.

During the shift on a job the driver could not smoke a pipe; it
was a hazard where sudden physical responses may be called for
at any moment. And they disdained cigarettes; only a dude or a
freight wagon driver or a maverick of similar lower caste would
condescend to the use of such sissy trifles. No, a good cigar was
the thing. A popular driver's daily supply of expensive cigars
was constantly being replenished by grateful passengers who,
knowing that the offer of a tip would be haughtily declined, gave
the next best and always acceptable token of appreciation.

Sometimes their good fellowship was sharpened by serious
rivalry. Hank Monk was perhaps the kingpin of the drivers. His
reputation was deserved, but he also had an instinct for
theatrical public relations and was never bashful about tooting
his own horn. One night in Sonora he was telling for the
umpteenth time about when he had the famous editor Horace
Greeley as a passenger. The great man was scheduled to make a
speech in Placerville, and Monk had to get him there on time.
Because of rains, however, the stage was late and they had to

make up for lost time. Around the curves and over the bumps they went, with Greeley bouncing around in the coach. In discomfort and despair, Greeley begged the driver to slow down, but Hank only cracked his whip, yelled at his plunging team that spurted ahead like racehorses leaving the starting line, and shouted back to his notable guest: "Keep your seat, Horace! I'll get you there on time!" And he did. Later the famous editor wrote him up in the newspaper for it.

Charley was tired of the story. He only grunted, "Horace Greeley got what he deserved; he should have known better than to ride behind six plow horses and a jackass." The others laughed, but Charley rarely smiled. Although he would join the group and drink his share of beer with them, he always remained aloof and his occasional acid remarks were usually aimed at stopping a topic of conversation rather than adding to it.

One time in Jackson the boys were talking about a cargo of special passengers one of them had brought in. They were a small troupe of girls accompanied by their "manager" who escorted them from camp to camp for the purpose of putting on shows for the miners. They would dress in provocative costumes and sing and dance for the enjoyment of the saloon customers, and afterward they were free to pursue such other profitable enterprises as temptation might put in their way.

"That's one covey of quail you'd shore ought to see. They're really highfalutin'," one driver commented.

Parkhurst grunted but said nothing. Another driver, Watson by name, thought he would have a little fun on this salacious subject. "Hey, Charley," he taunted, "you ought to hook up with one of them pretty hurdy-gurdy girls and settle down. I hear they make good wives once you get 'em broke-in to a one-team harness." But Charley did not rise to the bait. The ensuing silence rankled Watson and he could not let the matter drop there. He turned to the other grinning members of the clan.

"Well, fellers, I guess old Charley ain't been wized up yet; his education seems to be limited to horses. Leastwise, he don't know much about women."

"You might be surprised," cracked Charley. "You don't know half as much as you think you do, yourself. If guts was brains you'd be a genius. But if it'll make you any wiser I'll buy the next round of beer." And that ended that conversation.

The hazards of driving were never taken lightly. Comfort and safety for the passengers and the faithful delivery of mail and express shipments were never forgotten. A station agent who dispatched a stage had to be alert for dangerous weather conditions, the possibility of washouts, and the likelihood that sooner or later some highwayman would be lurking at a sudden bend in the road with intent to lighten the burden of both coach and passengers. Prior to each departure the agent and driver would hold an informal conference on such matters.

On one occasion Charley was warned not to make the run because of the weather, but he chose to go anyway. That winter the snow pack in the mountains had been unusually heavy, and when spring came the runoff from the melting snow was filling the rivers. Recent heavy rains had made matters worse, and floods were inevitable. The Tuolumne River had swollen over its banks in the valleys and was savagely cutting away its walls in the canyons, roaring down like the boring force from a nozzle, bringing trees and other debris with it.

The bridge below Big Oak Flat was in danger of being washed out, and Charley knew that it was only a matter of time. He gave the horses their heads, and the coach careened down the narrow road toward the river. As they rounded a curve Charley and his one passenger could see the raging flood just below them. The bridge was about fifty yards away. Suddenly in the middle of the road ahead a stranger appeared, waving his arms and shouting against the roar of the torrent. Charley pulled the horses to a sliding stop.

"Leastwise, he don't know much about women."

"You better not try to cross that bridge," screamed the obviously frightened man. "She's about to go any minute!"

Charley looked at his passenger and then at the valuable express box he had to deliver.

"Don't go!" pleaded the passenger. "I can wait. We can't take the chance. Let's go back!"

The driver hesitated. The struggle was between common sense and honor. A tense instant of silence, and the decision was made. Charley let out a screeching Rebel yell, cracked the whip, and with a twist of the wrists took a double hitch on the reins. The little coach shot forward, down to the swaying bridge. With nostrils wide and ears back, the six horses hit the boards of the bridge almost as one. The wheels skidded as they made the curve and slammed onto the shuddering planks. Logs and brush had lodged against the bridge and water was beginning to rush over it.

The coach hurtled across and came to a stop on the other side. At that moment, with a squeaking cry the bridge tore from its moorings and was swept away in the foaming torrent. Charley and the passenger watched it go.

"Good Lord!" the passenger gasped in relief. "I thought we were goners for sure. Another second and we would have been down there in that water, me and you both."

"Aw, hell," snorted Charley. "I'd never let that happen. I'm particular who I take a bath with." The passenger and the strong box were delivered on time.

Calamities of nature were not the only hazards of the road. The drivers also had to contend with highwaymen. This was before the time of the notorious Black Bart, but even in these early days of stagecoach travel in the Mother Lode country there were holdup men who plied their trade with tolerable success. A few worked the same locality long enough to become known. One such character was an enterprising entrepreneur of the road who came to be called Sugarfoot. Not much is known about him, but in the folklore of the region it is said that on two occasions he and Charley Parkhurst came face to face in their respective occupations.

The first time, Charley was on the Mariposa-to-Stockton run and was carrying a large sum of gold in the strong box resting under the driver's seat. It was a hot summer day, and Charley's mind was probably on that cool glass of beer that awaited him in the next town rather than on the possibility of a holdup. Suddenly two bandits with faces covered stepped out from behind a large rock. One grabbed the lead horses, and the other leveled a double-barreled shotgun at Charley.

"Now, don't try to be a hero, Charley," the holdup man cautioned. "All we want is the box, so toss 'er down, and no foolishness about it."

"Foolishness, hell!" snorted Parkhurst. "I was asleep or you wouldn't of got this far. I take it you'd be Sugarfoot, you low-down..." The unprintable epithets were cut short by the bandit.

"You might be right. You just tell 'em old Sugarfoot got the last laugh on you this time."

"Well, this'll be the last time," mumbled Charley as he threw down the box. "Next time you try this on me, I'll put daylight through that yellow liver of yours, and that's no lie."

So the outlaws got the gold, and Charley smarted from the embarrassment of it. The next day he slipped a loaded pistol under the driver's seat, and thereafter never made a run without it.

A few months later the showdown came. On the same run and almost at the same place, again two masked gunmen suddenly appeared and waved the horses to a stop. The express box was carrying more gold than usual, and this time Parkhurst was not taken by surprise. The order was given to toss down the box. Pretending to comply, Charley reached down for the heavy chest; in the same apparently awkward movement he suddenly jerked on the reins. The lead team reared back and the other horses jostled in confusion. The distraction was momentary;

both bandits looked at the horses. Charley, stooping for the box, came up with the gun. Two quick shots cracked out. One outlaw dropped his shotgun and grabbed his stomach. The other dodged into the bushes, jumped on his horse, and clattered off up the rocky hillside.

The wounded man stumbled to his horse and managed to get away, but a few days later he was found in an abandoned miner's cabin not far away, dying. He was identified as Sugarfoot.

At one stage in his career—some said it happened near Redwood City—Parkhurst met with the kind of accident that all drivers dreaded. He was kicked in the face while trying to shoe a horse. He lost the sight of his left eye, and for the rest of his life he wore a patch over it. From then on people called him "One-Eyed Charley," but not in his presence, of course.

In 1867 Charley established his final residence in Santa Cruz County. Accordingly, he registered his citizenship there as Charley Darkey Parkhurst, age 55, occupation farmer, native of New Hampshire, residence: Soquel. There is no evidence to show whether the middle "Darkey" was a family name or a pejorative epithet, but apparently it was legal enough; he voted in the 1868 national election.

Aging or used-up stage drivers had no future to look forward to, and as it must to all men the time finally came to retire. Rheumatism had made Charley's driving difficult, wages were going down, and he began to think of a better life. With his savings he was able to buy a small ranch near Soquel and raised apples, wheat, hay, and a few cattle. But the increasing pain of rheumatism and a rapidly developing cancer of the tongue rendered him helpless, and he had to sell the ranch. He moved to a small cabin near Watsonville, where kind friends could look in on him occasionally.

He had lived a most colorful life. Known far and wide as one of the best whips of the Gold Rush days, he had enjoyed the professional respect of his peers. He had killed an outlaw and thus had gained a moment of fame. He had rolled dice for the drinks, chewed tobacco, smoked cigars, and gambled in the saloons with the toughest of his kind. Yet he was fiercely independent and refused medical aid even in the last painful days of his life. Despite his renown he was always a loner and seemed to relish the shadows of mystery that enveloped him.

He died alone, and his secrets followed him almost to the grave. But when George Harmon discovered the small twisted body and the coroner was called, his greatest secret was revealed. Charley Parkhurst was a woman.

The Case of
Vallejo *vs.* El Azucarero

HE WAS ONLY a little Frenchman but he had big ideas. One in
particular was a grand idea. In fact, it was the kind of vision that
every lazy man was fed upon—the dream of the Big Rock Candy
Mountain. But why not? It is the lazy man who learns to use his
head, to find the easy way to live; thus many great discoveries have
been made. Little Octavio Custot knew this. "My *grandpère*, he say
this to me," and the Frenchman tapped the side of his head
knowingly, "he say to me: 'The head, thees *extrémité supérieure*,
she is to save the heels.'" And so, with this grand old idea that the
head should save the heels, Octavio Custot came to California.

General Mariano Vallejo, the highly respected and prosperous
Mexican governor of northern California, and the diminutive
Octavio Custot, who had come to California to find an easy and
prosperous life, stood together on the gentle slope from the south
side of the massive adobe and looked down across the vast spread
of land that the General claimed as part of his Petaluma ranch. The
grass was dry now, for it was mid-summer, but the earth lay rich
under it. Vallejo believed in the land. In the Sonoma Valley his
vineyards had been fruitful, and in the hills the tall grass had
fattened his cattle. And here now, spreading before the two men,

was something that might be even more responsive to the General's touch.

"Thees land, she will be very rich I think," said the Frenchman, and General Vallejo saw the dream. He saw, not the dry grass sloping off toward the Petaluma hills, but cultivated fields with rich green stripes that meant row after row of a field crop new to California. This vision that he saw was acres and acres of sugar beets fattening in the rich California soil.

The Frenchman had come with a new idea, like a stranger bearing gifts from a far-off land, and Vallejo had listened eagerly. The magic word was *sugar*. There was no sugar to be had in northern California. The sugar on the General's table came all the way from Peru, and it was expensive. Think of the fortune that could be made if someone only knew how to produce sugar here. Although the sorghum that was raised made good molasses, that was far from being refined sugar. But beets—now that was another matter. The General knew that in other parts of the world sugar was being made from a special kind of beet. This soil could grow that beet. And now this man, this stranger from Europe, knew the secrets of how to cultivate these beets and convert them into sugar. There was a fortune to be made from this enterprise—for Vallejo, at least—and the team of Custot and Vallejo could bring the plan into life.

But where were the seeds to come from? There were no beet seeds in California. "Send away for them, of course. It will take time, naturally, but time we 'ave," said the Frenchman. And time, indeed, Custot had, and even more time was what he most wanted. So an order was sent, not to Peru but to Mazatlan, for the precious seed of the sugar beets, and Custot settled down to wait.

Vallejo designated forty acres near the Petaluma hacienda for the new project, and Custot sat under a tree, and smoked, and studied the situation. Vallejo provided him with eight yokes of oxen and eight Indians to do the plowing; and while the slow, laborious work went on, Custot sat under his tree, and smoked, and studied the project more carefully. He lived as an honored guest at the adobe, which was as yet not quite finished in its half-completed compound; and he grew fat on the General's food. He danced at the fiestas and sang when he felt like it, he enjoyed the company of the travelers who stopped there, and he basked in the luxury of the patronage of the great Governor-General himself. What more could a man want?

In fact, this was exactly what Custot had ventured all the way to California to find. He had come on a trading ship to these western shores, presumably working his way as a sailor; but precious little work he did. Through trickery and flattery he managed to get the other sailors to do his work for him. When they landed in San Pedro he gambled for enough money to finance a glorious adventure in Los Angeles. And when his ship went to Monterey, his shore leave was again filled with the joy of mingling with the citizens. Here was a tranquil people. No one seemed to work but the Indians. There was always time to enjoy life, and there was always tomorrow for what needed to be done. This was the paradise he had been seeking. Here a man who hated work with a fierce revulsion could practice the art of indolence with dignity and respect. All he needed was his wits; California provided the rest.

So in Monterey he had jumped ship and slipped away to seek his placid fortune in the heart of this new land. He had gone inland and then drifted northward, finally coming to rest under the generous patronage of none other than the grandest gentleman of them all, Vallejo himself.

The simple ingenuity of his plan astonished even himself. He had seen sugar beets grow, and he knew that the precious sweet substance could be made from them. To arouse Vallejo's interest in the idea was a simple matter, and the result was *magnifique et phénomènal.* The American phrase "Big Rock Candy Mountain" was to come much later in the history of indolence, but he was familiar with the idea for which the French did have an appropriate expression. This was his "Castle in Spain."

He sat under his tree and pondered the matter, after which he rested. Meanwhile his faithful Indians guided the slow oxen up and down the fields turning over the rich earth. The summer wore away, and the soil was finally ready. But there was nothing that could be done. The seeds had not yet come. There was nothing to do but wait. Autumn slowly merged into winter, and the rains came. It was a long, slow, pleasant winter, and Octavio Custot enjoyed the leisure of it.

When the seeds finally arrived it was spring again. Custot studied the situation. Obviously the winter rains had packed the soil. The ground must be plowed again so the fine seeds could have a chance to sprout and grow. So the oxen and the plows and the Indians went to work again, and the brown earth was turned over once more.

But of course when this was finished it was summer again, and it was the considered advice of this French sugar expert that it would be better to wait until after the next rains; otherwise the fine seeds might be wasted. So Vallejo impatiently waited, eager for the crop that would bring him new wealth. And Custot waited, content in the luxury of his ease.

Eventually the seeds were planted. The beets grew and the fields were beautifully green. The beets were big in their soil, and Vallejo knew that the crop would yield a bounteous harvest. Custot spent a blissful summer and fall. He went to parties at Sonoma and even as far away as Yerba Buena across the bay. He was always made welcome, of course, and the entertainment was always splendid. He enjoyed the bullfights, the cockfights, the horse races, the fiestas. He saw and enjoyed his first rodeo. Life was wonderful in California.

When harvest time came, the General's interest in the beet crop increased. He also began to ask questions about how the beets were to be converted into sugar. "But *monsieur*, I am ze one to know this secret," Custot assured him. A large shed was provided, and certain items of machinery, pipes, and vats were ordered according to the Frenchman's specifications. But Custot refused to reveal the secret process or even allow anyone into his mysterious laboratory.

The beets were harvested and stored. Monsieur Custot went

into his shed, from which strange sounds and smells emanated, and the Vallejo family waited. Two years had passed, and they had been good, fat years for the clever Frenchman. Now the moment of truth was at hand.

The Vallejos did not actually live at the Petaluma adobe, but they frequently came over from Sonoma to spend a few days at a time to enjoy the ranchero and supervise the building of the compound around the adobe.

On this occasion, the unveiling of the sugar, the General and Doña Francesca Vallejo, accompanied by several members of their family and household, had come, and a sumptuous dinner was ordered. The meal was served without the presence of Custot; he had sent his apologies, saying that he would be a little late because of unexpected developments in his laboratory. When he finally arrived, he made a grand entrance, bringing with him that miracle of miracles, a box of sugar. It was a loaf of the finest sugar the General had ever tasted. All agreed that it was fully as good as the best Peruvian cane sugar. In fact, it tasted very much like the best Peruvian cane sugar. That evening the great landowner made plans to have a million acres planted with beets the next year— well, at least a hundred acres.

Monsieur Custot did not enjoy the dinner as much as usual. He seemed worried about something. After dinner Doña Francesca and an Indian servant took the remainder of the treasured loaf of sugar to the store room to put it away. It was to be placed beside the other boxes of sugar that had been shipped from Peru. But when they went to put it on the shelf they made a strange discovery. One box of the imported sugar was missing.

The logical-minded lady stormed back into the dining hall and bluntly accused the Frenchman of stealing her sugar. The General knew immediately what had happened and his anger flared. He demanded to see how this expert on sugar actually made the product.

"I am afraid, *monsieur,*" said the troubled Frenchman, "that you will not learn much about it. You see, I am very sorry, but I do not know how to make the sugar." The General exploded. The unhappy culprit waited meekly for the guillotine to fall.

The General called for his Indian aide, Chief Solano, a giant creature completely loyal to his patron and devoted to the Vallejo family. He gladly would have killed anyone who offended the General, but it would be a particular pleasure to eliminate this wily foreigner whom he hated. The General ordered Solano not to kill him, as the Indian hoped, but merely to run him off the place. The sentence, then, was to be exile.

Custot apparently did not repent his crime nearly as much as he regretted having to leave his happy home. These had been two of the pleasantest and laziest years of his inactive life, and the thought of being expelled from this Garden of Eden made him shudder. Oh, well, he shrugged; it had been good while it lasted.

The Indian Solano took charge of his prisoner with military efficiency. The next morning he thrust the unhappy Frenchman into a cart and wheeled him to the landing place on the Petaluma River. There he dragged him into a large boat, and with Indians at the oars they went down the river and across the bay. When they came within sight of the shore they observed that the tide was out and hence could not approach the dock at Yerba Buena. Solano stopped the boat some three hundred yards from shore.

The little Frenchman argued, threatened, cajoled, and begged, but the stubborn Indian refused to move any closer. This development was a pleasant one for Solano, and his enjoyment increased as he observed how frightened his victim was. He made a threatening gesture, and the terrified Custot tumbled into the water and began to wade ashore.

He slogged through the wide slough of soft mud. Slimy, dirty, and miserable, the poor fellow dragged himself ashore where he was met by a crowd of people who had been watching the proceeding with considerable interest. It had been supposed that he was the bearer of an important message and had rushed ashore to deliver it because there had been no time to await the rising tide. But, alas, the little fellow had no message. Nor did he receive the welcome that he had enjoyed when he was part of the powerful Vallejo household.

And thus it was that the clever Frenchman, Monsieur Octavio Custot, returned to a well-earned world of nothingness. History does not follow his idle existence beyond this point. But he was remembered long afterward by the Indians and Mexicans of the Vallejo family. They always laughed when they thought of him, and they called him *El Azucarero*, The Sugar Maker, because he could not make sugar.

Who Killed Juanita?

You might call it a lynching. Or you might call it a legal execution by the State of California. In 1851 that was a distinction that made little difference—to the accused, anyway. But it has become a local legend that is perhaps as much the story of an early-day mining camp as it is about the principal characters.

The Fourth of July came early to Downieville that year. You could hardly say that the festive drinking started early, for such patriotic and manly expressions of zeal continued unabated throughout the year. But plans for the special holiday had started sooner than usual. The idea that, of all the mining camps in the northern Sierra, Downieville must have the grandest celebration was an inspiration that had taken root, and its growth was phenomenal. It had borne fruit ahead of time, and by the first of July the town was ready.

A platform decked with flags had been built to elevate the orators and provide visible seating for the local dignitaries. Colored cloth had been improvised to simulate gala decorations over the platform, and wildflowers and evergreen boughs of pine and fir had been strewn around the little park to add an esthetic touch. The local five-piece band had practiced its repertoire of three rousing tunes, one for marching into the arena, one to render as a classical interlude between the speeches, and one for a recessional.

Two highly renowned speakers, one from Sacramento, had been selected to declaim the usual platitudes of patriotism, which would be more stirring this year because it was 1851 and California had just become a state. Other mining camps might have one orator, but Downieville could settle for no less than two. The speakers would be expected to describe in graphic detail how the noble forefathers of the Republic fought for freedom and justice; and they would be wildly applauded for revealing that the hand of God aided in their heroic struggles against aggression, and that California was to be the shining example of virtue in protecting the divine rights of the most lowly of her citizens. Such truths would be proclaimed as if from the pulpit and would be as devoutly accepted.

That the celebration was to last three days, culminating in a climactic finale on the Fourth was a welcome development. The miners and loggers could thus prolong their bacchanalian devotions, enjoy more fights, and savor such other manly sports as circumstances might permit.

Today, the visitor to Downieville, high in the Sierra Nevada Mountains north of Grass Valley and Nevada City, will find a quiet, peaceful, quaint, picturesque little village. It nestles deep in the hills, with a few of the original old houses still clinging to the rugged canyon walls. Through its center cuts one of the most delightful streams to be found anywhere in the world. This is the upper branch of the Yuba River, which drops down through the steep, rough canyon below. Today the town is a sleepy mountain retreat.

But in the 1850s the story would be quite different. It was the meanest, toughest, wildest, drinkingest, most rambunctious town in all the northern gold country. The mining camps in the Sierra were all rough, but this was the roughest. And those beautiful hills were so rugged that even the trail leading into the town was treacherous. It was so narrow and dangerous in places that many people actually lost their footing and slipped off, dropping to their death on the jagged rocks below.

The peaceful little Yuba River in flood time could become a raging, vicious, devastating torrent. And the people who lived there resembled the stream. On Sunday afternoons those miners might be seen in their loud red shirts—now clean after the Saturday night bath—sitting in the restaurant at tables with checkered tablecloths and using napkins as politely as you please. But later they would go across the river to the saloon and drink so hard and fast—so it has been said—that sometimes they wouldn't even bother to pull the corks out of the bottles. They just broke their necks—of the bottles, that is—and gulped the contents without ceremony or delay.

Anyone who didn't drink in Downieville was regarded as a suspicious character. Yet only a few miles away was Poker Flat, the town that local legend identifies with the scene of Bret Harte's famous story, "The Outcasts of Poker Flat," where piety drove out the evil element and the winter storms did the rest. This is only the fiction of local pride, of course; there is another place in the Mother Lode country that also claims to be the real Poker Flat.

The nature of Downieville, human and otherwise, was a story of conflict between extremes. The same people at different times and in varying moods found ways to express the alternating opposites of beauty and ugliness, good and evil, decorum and violence. Such ambivalence may help to explain a chain of events that occurred there on that Fourth of July which sickened the state, horrified the nation, and shocked the world.

Even the elements seemed to take a hand, and the ill-fated bridge where the story reached its climax was destroyed by floods the following spring. It was an episode that got into poetry and song, and it still lies deep in the memories of people who have lived there and heard the story these many generations later. It is a legend now, but it was once the true story of a Mexican girl named Juanita.

The Fourth of July went off as expected. But after three days of celebration the participants were beginning to run out of ideas for excitement and diversion. An anti-climax was setting in. Something had to be done to liven up the situation.

One of the leading revelers was a fellow named Jack Cannon, a big handsome Scotsman. He was the envy of all the miners in camp who thought they were strong, and a hero to the rest. Being a leader among men, Cannon naturally became the inspiration of a little band of rioters who decided it would be a great diversion in the middle of the night to go around the village and burst open the cabin doors and rouse the sleeping people. This proved to be hilarious sport, and as they went from house to house waking and frightening the bewildered occupants their fun increased.

Down at the end of town, however, there was one cabin where they were not welcome. It was the house of the Mexican girl, Juanita. When they kicked open the door and started into the house they were faced by an angry woman, a very fireball of a woman, who shouted a high-pitched volley of Spanish words at them which they could not understand, and kicked them on the legs and slapped their faces—which they could understand. They retreated in some disorder.

Juanita was a very beautiful young woman. She had the Mexican dark eyes and long black hair. She was small and well-shaped and was blessed with that vivaciousness and physical vitality that made it pleasant and exciting to be near her. But she also had a fiery temper. It was rumored, sometimes to her credit and sometimes not, that she was not as good a girl as she should be, but the miners admired her. It is likely that many of them were privately in love with her, and perhaps some of them felt secretly guilty about their feelings.

On this occasion her hostility came as a surprise. Her resistance spoiled the sport and frustrated the carousers. Cannon and his gang of hoodlums backed off in confusion and went their way, by this time pretty well sobered up. Then, according to subsequent testimony, later that morning Jack Cannon and a friend of his went back to Juanita's house for reasons that were never made quite clear. Some said it was to apologize for his behavior of the night before; others said he went back for less honorable reasons. At any rate, he and his friend returned to Juanita's place and this time knocked on the door.

After much knocking and a long wait, they heard movement within. The door was opened and again the young woman stood before them, still in a rage. Behind her, in the shadows of the room, they saw another person. It was her Mexican boyfriend, who apparently was there to protect her. The talk was in Spanish, which Cannon's friend could not understand, but he could tell that they were very angry.

Cannon knew a few words of Spanish, and it was said that he made some very insulting remarks. His companion saw Juanita step away and disappear into the back of the house. Cannon still stood in the door talking to her Mexican friend, with his big hands against the two sides of the door frame.

Suddenly Juanita appeared again. She approached with one hand behind her back. She pushed past her friend and came straight up to Cannon. In a flash she brought her hand around, and in it she was clutching a long knife. Without a word she plunged the knife deep into his breast. He fell, and bled, and quickly died.

The news spread, and immediately a crowd gathered. Cannon the bully had suddenly become very popular, and the crowd grew angry. Juanita sensed the feeling of the men, and with her friend slipped out of the house and went to Craycroft's saloon where she hid in the back room. The maddened crowd surrounded the saloon, and voices began to cry out for vengeance. The girl and her friend were dragged out and taken over to the flag-draped platform that had been erected in the plaza for the patriotic speakers the day before.

A court was quickly organized and twelve jurors selected. The Mexican friend was released, but Juanita was to have a trial. One doctor, a friend of hers, tried to speak on her behalf. He testified that she was going to have a baby and hence, according to the code of the West, she must be treated with consideration. But he was discredited; three other doctors were on hand to contradict his testimony.

A young lawyer in the crowd stepped up to try to defend her. He was a newcomer to Downieville, a tenderfoot who had just come from the States. He got up on a barrel and pleaded most earnestly that it would be a miscarriage of justice to convict her on the evidence presented, and a lasting shame on the town if they lynched a woman. But the crowd was angry. They jeered him for his efforts, and finally someone kicked the barrel out from under him, sending him sprawling. His hat went one way, his spectacles went another, and he was jostled out of the crowd.

But in all other respects the trial proceeded according to law. The judge was a duly authorized Justice of the Peace, and the prosecutor was elected by popular vote. The jury was drawn by lot from names in a hat. Witnesses were called and they solemnly swore to tell the truth, the whole truth, and nothing but the truth. Cannon's friend gave his version of the story. Expert medical testimony was given both as to the cause of death and the physical condition of the defendant.

The body of Cannon was laid before the court as evidence that all could see. One or two bold souls came forward to vouch for the girl's generally good character, but several others told the court what a "good old boy" Jack Cannon had been. He might have been a little wild at times, but "he never had a mean bone in his body." Juanita scorned the court and refused to speak in her own defense.

The case was heard, and the jury quickly brought in the verdict—guilty. Juanita was to be hanged for the murder of Jack Cannon. They gave her an hour to think things over and make her peace. She asked for a priest, but the request was denied, possibly because there was no priest to be found. She was put in the back room of the saloon, where she sat still and stared at the sullen faces of the men who had been left to guard her. Nothing needed to be said; her looks were eloquent in defiance and scorn.

When her hour was over, she was marched down the road to

the Jersey Bridge that crossed the river in the center of town. Planks had been arranged on the bridge and tied with ropes to form a platform on which she was to stand. As she was led to it, she saw her friend standing in the crowd below. She took off her hat and tossed it to him, and he silently clutched it to his breast.

The noose was ready, but the long black hair down her back was in its way. Eyewitnesses reported that she stood defiantly, and with great calm reached up and moved her beautiful hair aside for the adjustment of the rope. When everything was ready she spoke her last words in her own language: "Goodbye, friend." The word was given. A pistol was fired. The ropes were cut, and the planks dropped. Death came quickly for Juanita. And California had executed its first woman.

The whole world heard about the hanging from the Jersey Bridge in Downieville, but such news stories are quickly forgotten outside the region. But those who witnessed the event could not forget it. Several accounts were later written down, and at least one man published his verses about it—George Barton, who must have been there to see it with his own eyes. He wrote:

> She viewed the scene of hate and strife,
>   Heard maddened voices cry aloud
> That she must die, and life for life
>   Seemed the watchword of the crowd.
>
> With hurried forms they held the court,
>   The judge elected, jury sworn;
> It seemed but as a mocking sport,
>   For she would die before the morn.
>
> Was there no man dared to defend,
>   And help, a woman's life to save?
> A stranger tried, a humane friend—
>   He sank beneath that angry wave.

> And pity dwelt in scarce an eye—
>   But silence! Hear the verdict read:
> The prisoner's GUILTY, and must die—
>   Hung by the neck till she is dead.
>
> Bravely she climbed the fatal pile;
>   To one she knew, with graceful bend,
> Flung him her hat, and with a smile,
>   *"Adios, Amigo!"*—Good Bye, Friend.

Whether Juanita was legally executed or was lynched became a moot question at the time. It is still a question.

Kissane

"IF THAT OLD HOUSE could talk, what tales it could tell!" Such a conjecture can lay no claim to originality; it is often said, and is always worthy of speculation. Such a place is one of Sonoma County's most stately old mansions, Temelec Hall, which hides among the trees at the end of a long lane near the road from Sonoma to Petaluma. It was built in 1858 by Captain Granville Swift, a California pioneer who used Indian slave labor in a variety of profitable though shamefully cruel and illicit enterprises.

But despite its unholy origin the old home has stood in dignity and grandeur these hundred years and more, an eloquent reminder of the days of splendor and gracious living in California. And it has kept its secrets, particularly those about an honorable gentleman who owned the home, lived in it with dignity and splendor, and found there a sanctuary from the conflicts of the world from 1863 to 1887.

He enjoyed nearly a quarter of a century of quiet country life there, admired as a leader in the community and envied for his wealth, his gentlemanly elegance, and his personal charm. No country squire ever enjoyed more respect from the gentry around him. This was Colonel William K. Rogers, generous patron of good causes and wise counselor to all who sought his help. But hidden beneath this noble exterior an altogether different kind of man was imprisoned. The real Colonel Rogers was in fact one of the most ruthless criminals of his time, with innocent blood on his hands and stolen gold in his pockets, and his name was Kissane.

In 1863 the Civil War was still raging. People were flocking to California, some to escape the war, some to rest and settle down after having served their country on either side of the conflict and were simply tired of fighting, and some without reference to the war at all but only to make money. Colonel Rogers never got around to explaining why he was in California, but he had been here a year or two before settling in Sonoma County. It was said that he made his money in the excitement at Gold Hill, where fortunes in gold were indeed found, but no one knew for sure. Then in 1863, as a paradise for retirement, he selected the grand estate of the late Granville Swift and nestled down to live in peace and respectability.

At last, on an evening in May, 1887, an officer of the Federal Court knocked on the front door of this country home. The door was opened by Colonel Rogers himself. He stood tall and straight. His face was sun-browned and wrinkled. His hair and moustache were snow-white, his eyebrows were bushy, and the cold gray eyes that met the visitor's inquiring look glared with a hawk-like fierceness.

The officer said, "I have papers from the United States Federal Court which I wish to serve on William Kissane." The defiant eyes closed for an instant, and the hand that held the door trembled slightly. Then the Colonel said calmly, "Drive around to that clump of eucalyptus and I will send him to you." The officer withdrew to the little grove of trees behind the mansion and waited. Before long the man who had met him at the door joined him.

"I thank you, sir," said the Colonel. "I am William Kissane." The officer handed him a summons to appear in court and answer to charges for a crime committed thirty years before. The Colonel acknowledged the serving of the paper, and then he said, "Please excuse my not asking you into the house. But you see, we are all—the family, that is—I trust you will pardon me, sir."

The visitor took his leave and the Colonel walked slowly back across the lawn and entered the house. His past had finally overtaken him, and he was ready now to go to San Francisco for the trial he had always known must come. He was no longer Rogers the country gentleman, but Kissane the criminal who knew very well the ways of the law.

His memory flashed back to a famous trial in 1853 in Columbus, Ohio. He had been acquitted then, but the case had stirred the morbid imagination of the whole world. It had been the notorious *Martha Washington* case in which he and other defendants had enlisted the aid of the keenest legal minds in America to get them off.

A river steamer called the *Martha Washington* had left the Cincinnati docks late on the night of January 7, 1852. She was heavily freighted with a cargo consigned to New Orleans and the markets of Texas and California. The cargo was an immense load of leather goods, sheepskins, boxes of boots, candles, pork, whiskey, brandy, and barrels of oil. The shipment was heavily insured at a figure far greater than the goods were worth, and the ship was also insured. Kissane and his partners held the insurance, and the plan was to burn the vessel and collect on both ship and cargo.

It had been an unusually cold winter, and river traffic on the Ohio River had been stalled in ice for some time. The *Martha Washington* was the first steamer to go down the river after the breaking of the ice, and to the surprise of the conspirators thirty people bought passage on the ill-fated ship. There was no way to refuse them transportation without arousing suspicion, so they were taken aboard.

The freighter nosed its way carefully down the Ohio and entered the Mississippi. It was the seventh day out, and the night was the coldest the river men could remember. In some mysterious way the ship caught fire and burned to the water's edge and sank. Passengers and crew in panic leaped into the freezing river. Sixteen never reached shore.

The cargo was lost and the insurance was collected, and the families of the sixteen mourned their dead. The crime might never have been detected if a man named Thomas Burton had not, quite by chance, discovered in a warehouse some of the skins that were claimed to have been lost in the disaster. Investigation then revealed that the boxes supposedly containing boots and shoes were filled with scraps of old leather, sand, and sawdust, and the reputed barrels of oil and brandy were nothing more than so much water.

Kissane and his fellow conspirators were quickly brought to trial. Five weeks the case lasted, during which time the members of the jury were secretly threatened, bribed, or more subtly influenced by the beautiful feminine sympathizers of the accused. Political pressure was also brought into the trial, for Kissane and his friends were not without power in high places. The jury finally brought in a verdict of "Not Guilty," and, for a short time at least, Kissane was free.

Free, but not safe! Some of the relatives of the sixteen victims took an oath of vengeance to exact justice where the courts had failed; and one by one those who had shared his guilt and stood trial with him met with fatal accidents or disappeared without a trace. Always alert, Kissane managed to avoid these sinister shadows of revenge, but his other nemesis was the law. He was soon arrested again, this time for forgery. Again there was a trial, but unlike the other it was swift and quiet and he was convicted.

While being taken from jail to the courthouse to be sentenced, with the aid of some outside help, he overpowered his guards and escaped. The hue and cry went out, and the police tightened their net around Cleveland. In a few days, in the rural outskirts of the city, he was caught disguised as an ox-driver riding on a wagon load of freight and urging his plodding beasts along a back road. But the law could not hold him. Once again he managed to escape.

In 1854 he showed up in New York. Under an assumed name there he worked out one of the most elaborate and clever swindles of the decade. With some stolen check blanks, a little skillful forgery, and a series of minor transactions in which he built up his credit and made friends in the Chemical Bank of New York, he once again, with the help of an accomplice, got away with several thousand dollars. For some reason he then headed back to Ohio.

Back home he was caught again and returned to New York for trial. On the train he managed to give his guards the slip and made a daring escape that would stretch the credibility of even a movie writer. Again the chase was on, and again he was captured. In New York the wheels of justice turned fast. He was tried and this time the jury took only ten minutes to bring in a verdict of guilty. But when he stood up for sentence Kissane was ready for his real fight. He made a plea for mercy that was so eloquent, his story was so sad, and his expressions of guilt and remorse so stirring that the spectators were moved to tears and the judge melted in sympathy. He gave Kissane the minimum sentence.

After nine months he was pardoned. The governor had been overwhelmed with petitions from persons of national importance in his behalf. People formed groups to manifest their sympathy, and letters poured in. There were enough petitions and letters to make a large volume, and one of the most earnest of these pleas was from no less a personage than the prestigious Horace Greeley.

Free once again, Kissane left the country. He joined the Walker expedition to Nicaragua, which was made up for the most part of what were called "men of strong character, tired of the humdrum of common life." They were a band of adventurers and filibusterers invading a helpless foreign country with the sanction and flag of the United States, and Kissane found the situation just to his liking. He arrived in Nicaragua in February, 1856.

William Walker, who tried to conquer Nicaragua and Honduras (1855-1860), was a self-made military adventurer. Originally from Tennessee, with a degree in medicine, he found doctoring too dull and unrewarding. He practiced law briefly in Marysville, California, and then went to Mexico to attempt to establish a military colony in Sonora. His more lofty dream of power in Central America came from Cornelius Vanderbilt, who saw an opportunity to establish a new trade and migration route from the East Coast to California. During the Gold Rush, people who did not have time to travel around Cape Horn took the short-cut across the Isthmus of Panama. Vanderbilt secured a treaty with Nicaragua to set up a competing route for passengers and trade, but the idea was beset with problems—economic, political, and logistical—and Vanderbilt backed away from the project.

But Walker saw the chance he wanted. With a band of "fifty-six immortal" filibusterers he entered Nicaragua with the sanction of one of the political factions there and was given the rank of Colonel. He quickly seized control, made himself a general, consolidated his pillaging activities, and planned a coup that would have made him the dictator-president of the country. His regime in the form of a trade treaty was actually recognized in 1856 by President Franklin Pierce. Although he failed and was executed by a firing squad in Honduras in 1860, at the time our man Kissane joined him he was at the height of power.

Under an assumed name Kissane was ready for a fresh start. With his unfailing charm he quickly ingratiated himself with the officers and was soon appointed assistant in command with the rank of Major. He was put in charge of the army commissary, a job for which he had great natural talent. He showed such ability and devotion to duty that General Walker promoted him, and for eight months he had in his hands the entire finances of the country.

When General Walker was away from headquarters on expeditions, Kissane made raids on neighboring haciendas, confiscating property and holding the wives and children of prominent Nicaraguans for ransom. It was reported that he made a large fortune in the sale of property he had seized. Under his direction cathedrals, convents, and private dwellings were pillaged of gold, silver, and jewelry. His plunder, it was said, filled six large cedar chests.

He shipped this treasure to New Orleans for safekeeping to be claimed later. But this was too good to last. He was suspected, but no one could prove his guilt; the men who had acted under his command were either shipped out or met with fatal accidents. Then quite by chance one day he was recognized. A young man from the States who knew him as Kissane happened to meet him on the street and called him by name. Since Kissane could not afford to have his true identity revealed, something had to be done. On that same night, by some strange coincidence, the young man was killed in an alley by persons unknown.

When the Nicaragua campaign collapsed it was time for Kissane to move on, covering his tracks behind him. To close that chapter completely he caused to be published in the papers a notice of his death. According to the glowing account, his demise was most heroic. So, thus safely dead, he was able to escape to Panama. From there he went to China and took part in the Taiping Rebellion—on the winning side, of course. His shrewdness soon secured him the favor of the Emperor, and he gained the rank of General.

Before the close of the rebellion, however, he left China to reappear briefly pursuing pleasure in the capitals of Europe. Finally, he drifted to California, where his mother and brother had gone to live. To avoid the stigma of their name, they had changed their identities and were good honest citizens of San Francisco, where the brother practiced as a lawyer.

Kissane then went to British Columbia. There on the Fraser River, three thousand miles from railroad and telegraphic communications, he felt safe. It was not the law he feared now, but the vengeance of those he had wronged.

Gold had been discovered on the Fraser River, and Kissane knew how to get his share of it. Everything he touched, it seemed, turned to profit. Just how he got it this time no one knows, but when he came back to civilization again he had several bags full of the precious dust. This time he went to Sacramento where he invested in real estate, and again he prospered.

Then, after a successful venture in mining, probably at Gold Hill, he decided to retire. With his tremendous fortune, no new crimes were necessary for him and the ghosts of his old crimes were following wherever he went. Somewhere, sometime, he was sure to be recognized. He never knew when someone might be waiting for him with a gun or knife to even the score on some old wrong. He yearned for safety and respectability, and above all he wanted to find a haven where he could live in quiet luxury.

Temelec Hall was just such a place. Here at last, hidden away in the remote countryside, was home. The sweet smell of the wisteria in summer, the cool shade of the magnolia trees, the music of the stream that ran through his back yard, and the vineyards that spread down to the valley—these were his reward now.

The people knew and accepted him as Colonel William K. Rogers. Here he could raise his family. Just when he married we do not know, but he and his wife Elizabeth found Temelec a fertile place for the growing of grapes and the begetting of children. According to old account books, in 1876 his farm yielded 25,000 gallons of wine and 800 gallons of brandy. And according to informants relying on their memories the Rogerses had eight children. By what year this was accomplished we do not know, but it is said that some of their descendants still live in Sonoma County and are respected by our informants as being "some of the finest people in the county." The large family, many loyal friends, and lavish entertainment made the grand old hall famous in the region. And the years rolled by.

But fate was not to be cheated of its prey. What finally led to his discovery was one of those ironies that only fate can devise. It was in 1879, and he had been in retirement sixteen years. General Ulysses S. Grant, former President of the United States, was visiting California as part of a tour of the world. He had gone from San Francisco to Sacramento by river boat and was returning to the Bay City by stagecoach.

It was a long drive that involved several stops. The secret service men were going ahead selecting places for the General to stay overnight, and it happened that the best resting place for the famous man was in Sonoma. What better accommodation could be found than the hospitable mansion of Colonel Rogers? Accordingly, a courier came to Temelec to ask whether the former President could be put up for the night.

To the agent's surprise Rogers declined the honor of entertaining such a guest. He explained that he did not have room to accommodate the party, but the real reason, of course, was his fear that someone in the General's entourage might recognize him. Such a chance he could not afford to take. But the machinery of fate had thus been set in motion; his refusal caused secret service men to wonder why. Questions were asked, and an investigation began.

Finally, the pieces were put together and the Federal officers identified Rogers as Kissane. The Chemical Bank of New York still had a claim against him, as did others he had swindled. So in 1890 Kissane, alias Rogers, went to San Francisco for trial. His brother, being a lawyer, was able to secure the best legal talent available to work in his behalf.

Once again the court ruled in his favor. The statute of limitations saved him; his crimes had been committed too long ago, and he could no longer be punished. But this time the ordeal proved too much for the old man. He came back to the mansion broken in health and spirit. In the long twilight after that, he would just sit on the veranda hour after hour, day after day, without speaking; he was only looking. Always he looked across the green vineyards below, but no one knew whether he was seeing their beauty.

In 1872 the place was heavily mortgaged, and in 1893 passed to other hands for debts that could not be paid. The family moved away, and ultimately Colonel Rogers was taken to a place where kind servants could help him die. And the grand old hall stood empty, neglected, unvisited, and alone, with its secrets hidden in a box of papers in the basement.

Peter Lassen

THEY HAD COOKED their supper over the bed of coals and hot ashes made by the soft, fast-burning butts of the sagebrush and had made sure that the saddle horses and pack animals were securely staked. Then the three men piled more sagebrush on the fire and settled down to smoke and talk. It was a snappy-cold evening in mid-April, and the desert turned quickly from warm to chilly almost as soon as the sun went down.

Old man Wyatt was in his middle sixties, and although he was big, weighing over two hundred pounds, he had long since given up the pretense of favoring the rugged life of the prospector. So without apology or explanation he draped a blanket over his shoulders and placed his saddle to lean against, and sat down to as much comfort as he could manage. Peter Lassen was fifty-nine and still had the iron of the blacksmith and fire of adventure in him. His Danish pride in physical fitness prevented him from relaxing into the lazy comfort that his tired bones ached for, and he squatted near the fire bareheaded and without the benefit of the heavy coat that was still strapped to his saddle. The other man, Clapper, stood by the fire and looked up at the sky as the coming darkness brought the stars into clear, vivid, brilliant focus.

It was 1859, and the three men were far out in the Black Rock Desert of Nevada. Nearly one hundred forty miles behind them was Susanville, and home. Somewhere before them lay the rugged ledges of Black Rock where the Lost Hardin mine was supposed to be. The three were on their way to find that mine, and at least one of them, Peter Lassen, was supposed to know just about where it was. He had even claimed to have a secret map, but if he did it was well hidden from the others.

"Them stars shore air purty," said Clapper. "Heard a feller say once that if'n you could read 'em right, them stars could tell you just about anything. Even like when you was supposed to die."

"Ve die when the time comes," Lassen said, almost to himself. And Wyatt reached for his rifle. He carefully scratched at a discolored splotch on the stock where the sweat and leather from his horse had rubbed, and said nothing. But Clapper was in a talkative mood.

"They say a feller remembers his whole life jest a-fore he dies. Now, take you, Peter. You've done a lot of things since you come to Californy. What would you think on, was you about to git called up?"

"Oh, the big things and the little things, some funny and some sad. But they all get mixed up, you know." And Lassen looked thoughtfully into the fire and began to remember things. There was the great dream he had had, the grand colony he had planned to build along the Sacramento River. He had conceived the idea first when he and John Bidwell were working for John Sutter. They were following horse thieves up the Sacramento Valley and had talked about the rich land and the good life to be found there. Peter Lassen—his real name was Lawson, but spelling gets changed in a new country—had secured his land grant from the Mexican governor in 1844, twenty thousand good acres beside the river. Then he had guided a party of immigrants to settle on his land, and he had called his town Benton City after Senator Benton, who was the father-in-law of John C. Fremont. Lieutenant Fremont had stopped at his place for awhile with his soldiers in 1846 just before

California was won from Mexico, and Lassen had felt a little pride in the fact.

He also remembered how his broad acres lay warm under the sun, and there was life in the rich earth. He remembered when he had cattle, horses and mules, sheep, and hogs. And he owned a fine big mill. These were all gone now, but the people had been proud to know him in those days. And he remembered how he had brought the first grape vines into the northern valley, and how his vineyards had prospered—for a time. Yes, he had led the party of immigrants into California and had shown them the good land. Now they owned the ranches and were prosperous, while he, their leader, had grown poor.

"Yah," he said, more to himself than to his companions. "I t'ink the people were glad I lead them to this country."

"Oh, I heard about you guidin' that party in over the Lassen Trail, only you just about didn't get 'em here. Tell me, Peter, was you lost most of the way, like they said?" Clapper wanted to know.

And Wyatt put in, "Course he was lost. They might of named that trail for him, but the way it zig-zagged around in them mountains folks said he was steering by a different set of landmarks every day."

"Hey, Peter," taunted Clapper with a broad grin, "I heered that you was so long gettin' 'em through and was so lost most of the time that them immigrants got you under a tree and was about to string you up. That so?"

"Vell, yes, they was pretty mad, you bet. I guess things looked pretty bad there for a little while. They do get the rope, and they do say they are goin' to hang me." And Lassen chuckled a little.

"Well, what happened?"

"Oh, they killed me, all right." Peter Lassen's grin broadened. Wyatt turned his attention back to the rifle he was cleaning. But Clapper wanted more.

"Hey, Peter," he went on, "You being such a pioneer and all, I expect you started a lot of things. I mean things that proved out successful."

Lassen thought again with pride of how he had brought the first charter for a Masonic Lodge to California. Maybe he hadn't been a successful rancher or guide, but he knew that he would be remembered for this, at least by those who cared. And those who loved the region might even remember that he had been elected president of he independent Territory of Nataqua. That had been a noble attempt to bring political order out of geographical chaos by claiming as a new state that vast region east of the Sierra Summit, which overlapped the country claimed by both California and Utah Territory. Right there in Isaac Roop's cabin in Susanville the boys had met and decided on having a free state—free from Brigham Young on one side and California on the other. Peter Lassen had presided at that historic meeting just three years ago, now. They were never able to establish any legal status for it, but the boys were willing to fight for it. And the fight wasn't over—not by a long shot.

Lassen enjoyed remembering those glorious days of inspiration and struggle. "Oh, I t'ink maybe I start a few things here, all right," he said.

"Yes, you shore did. Like maybe the time I heered when you went into the grindstone business, eh, Peter?" Clapper's leading question made Lassen's mind spin back to 1845, when he was just getting started in the Sacramento Valley. With William Moon and Ezekial Merritt he had decided to go into a business venture together. That was before Merritt had helped lead the Bear Flag Revolt that had resulted in the capture of General Vallejo, and the northern Mexican government, at Sonoma. Yes, they had gone into the grindstone business. They went over to Stony Creek, about thirty miles from the Sacramento River, and they quarried out some very good grindstones. They chiseled and shaped them, packed them on mules, and carried them back to the river, where they carefully loaded them on a little boat. In fact, they had put so many grindstones on the boat that the poor thing almost sank under the weight. When the tree men got aboard to float their cargo down the river, the water lapped over into the boat. They threw a few grindstones overboard and started down the river. It would have been a good bet that they wouldn't make it, but at every sizeable landing along the way they stopped and sold a grindstone or two—at a good discount, of course—in order to lighten the load. When they got to San Francisco Bay they had only a few grindstones left.

"Vell, ve didn't make much on the grindstones," chuckled Peter, "but ve sure had a fine big time of it when ve got to the city."

"I reckon I'd say as a river pilot you ain't no great shakes, either," said Clapper, who seemed interested in finding out just how far he could go in teasing the old man. Lassen had, as a matter of fact, tried his hand at navigation on the Sacramento River. In 1849 he had sold two thirds of his big ranch, giving the buyers easy credit on it. He received only $15,000 down, the balance to be paid in five years without interest. Then he had put all his cash into a steamboat. He had seen the river as a vital artery of transporation, and with his beautiful new steamboat which he called the *Lady Washington* he planned to go up and down carrying supplies to the settlers.

On his first trip out, he started from Yerba Buena loaded with merchandise and supplies. It took him and his crew about five months to maneuver the heavy vessel up the river. They were kept busy towing it over the rapids, pulling it around swift curves, dragging it out of constant entanglement with snags, and towing it backward off sandbars. In fact, the painful journey took so long that the crew ate up (or drank up) all the supplies, and he had nothing when he got home. To make matters worse, he found that thieves had stolen his cattle and he was faced with bankruptcy. So he sold the other third of the farm. The venture of his *Lady Washington* had been less than successful. But Lassen remembered the adventure with generous satisfaction.

"I did have a steamboat once," he said simply.

"Well, whatever became of her?"

"Oh, she blew up. And that was the long and short of it."

The sagebrush campfire had burned low, and Clapper reached for more fuel. Just then the horses lifted their heads and pricked up their ears. One of them gave a short, low whinny. The three men by the campfire sprang alert. There was something or someone out there on the desert. The men instinctively moved back from the fire and merged into the shadows around them. Clapper stepped over to the horses and gently patted one on the shoulder as he listened. Wyatt, holding his rifle in readiness, sidled over to the darkness of a bush nearby. Lassen stepped back with Wyatt. They waited, saying nothing.

In a moment a lone Indian entered the circle of light. He was obviously one of the Paiutes of the region. One thing you could always count on about the Paiutes: they were all destitute and always hungry, and from the white man would usually beg or more insistently demand whatever they needed at the time. This night visitor was true to form. He needed some ammunition for his old rifle. Clapper was all for running him out of camp and giving him nothing but a good scare. Wyatt, standing with his rifle at his hip and pointed toward the Indian, was for killing him then and there. But Lassen insisted upon feeding the poor fellow and giving him the ammunition he wanted. He had always been kind to the Indians, and they had come to call him "Uncle Peter." Many times he had defended them against the whites and had helped protect his friendly Indians against their enemies among their own people. He trusted them, and they had never betrayed his confidence. Now this lone Paiute took what he had come for and vanished into the darkness of the desert.

After he had gone, the three men speculated as to where he had come from and why he had been alone. He could have been sent to look over the camp to find out how many men and horses there were. Even if this were so, there was no way of knowing whether the Indians would attack or decide the odds were too great and move on. Or perhaps he was actually what he seemed to be, just a poor Indian.

"Nobody wants to kill me, I'm sure. Old Peter Lawson is friends to everybody," said Peter, and he settled down into his bedroll.

"Plenty of people could kill you," said Wyatt. "The Injuns ain't all your friends, and they'd like to get hold of these horses and our guns. Or maybe those people you sold your ranch to. No telling how much they owe you, and you without any wife or children to collect, they'd be right smart ahead if you never came back. Or some of those immigrants that almost strung you up might still have a grudge and come back to get you. Or even me," Wyatt added significantly. "If you have that map of the Lost Hardin Mine, like you claim to have, what's to keep Clapper and me from layin' you out right here and taking it all for ourselves? Or me alone, for that matter." And Wyatt placed his gun beside his bedroll.

"Well," said Clapper, "I reckon them big shinin' stars might know. But I shore as hell can tell you I don't, and I ain't worryin' much."

Peter Lassen merely said, "Now let's go to sleep." And the little campfire burned down, and the stars moved across the heavens, and Peter Lassen slept.

For what happened after that, we have only the word of old man Wyatt. A few days later he had ridden into Susanville alone with a strange story to tell. He described the camp the three prospectors had made that last night, and detailed the visiting of the Indian. He said that the next morning before they were awake and up, shots came in on them from two sides of the camp. Wyatt sprang up and Lassen grabbed his gun and cried, "You get the horses and put the stuff together; I'll fight them off." Wyatt found that the horses had been cut loose. As he was running to catch his own horse, he looked back and saw that Lassen had been shot. Clapper had been killed in his blankets with the first volley. Seeing that escape was his only hope, Wyatt ran, jumped on his horse, and rode bareback all the way back to Susanville.

He said it was Indians that had attacked them. Immediately a party of men from the Masonic Lodge went out to investigate. They buried Lassen and Clapper and examined all the evidence they could find. Wyatt had claimed that Indians had done it, but why would the Indians want to kill their friend? Chief Winnemucca said no, it wasn't the Indians. They all liked Uncle Peter. And if it had been Indians, they would have raided the camp. Yet the camp had not been disturbed. There was even a half barrel of whiskey sitting there, and it hadn't been touched. Surely if Indians had done it they would not have left the whiskey.

This was indeed a mystery. Yet no one in the community seemed to doubt Wyatt's story, at least openly, and no other suspect turned up, so the question was dropped. Later, Lassen's body was brought in and buried under a big pine tree near Susanville, and a marker was placed there to honor his memory. Who killed Clapper and Lassen, we'll never know. But everyone in northern California knows the name of Peter Lassen. A mountain, a county, and a national park bear his name, and he is remembered for many things. But as he said, "The big things and the little things—some are funny and some are sad. But they all get mixed up, you know."

Lieutenant Beale
and His Camels

A QUARTER OF A MILLION years ago—give or take a few years, more or less—native North American camels roamed this area. In the La Brea tar pits of Los Angeles, scientists have found some of their bones. And in a lava cave in southwestern Utah, a skull was found belonging to the same species. These bones were dated in the Pleistocene geologic period along with other interesting mammals of North America. But they have long been extinct, and this story is not about them.

In 1848 much of the western United States was considered the Great American Desert. No transcontinental railroad had been proposed—or even dreamed of by responsible people. But into and across this great desert, freight had to be moved. Army posts were scattered along important trailways, rivers, and strategic mountain passes. Immigrant parties were crawling westward in covered wagons. Settlements were taking root everywhere, and transportation was needed. The Army was charged with protecting these immigrants and settlers, and we are told that between 1844 and 1850, in those six years, the demand for Army mules increased ten times. It cost a lot of money to buy, feed, harness, and drive all these mules in these out-of-the-way desert and mountain outposts.

So in 1853 somebody came to Jefferson Davis with a fantastic idea. At that time he was Secretary of War for the United States, and one of his problems was to provide for the soldiers on the western frontier. This unusual idea showed imagination. In the Middle East, North Africa, and parts of Asia, people had been using camels for centuries to carry man and his burdens through the deserts. Why not do the same thing here? We could import camels, put them to work on our deserts, save the heavy cost of mules, and move a lot more freight faster with fewer animals.

Jefferson Davis accepted the idea. Many people laughed at him and called the project "Jeff Davis's Folly," but he had the courage to back his imagination. In 1855 he asked the Congress for $30,000 to buy camels. He sent buyers to the Levant, and in due time a shipment of camels arrived. They were landed at a seaport in Texas, and the plan was to test them out by bringing them across the southwest to California. It was midsummer, and they were to carry maximum loads. Some native camel drivers came along to teach the U.S. soldiers how to handle them.

Well, it wasn't long before trouble set in. The soldiers could talk to their Missouri mules in a language understood by both, and the mules would respond. But how can a camel from the Middle East understand a U.S. soldier? Or vice versa? They had nothing in common, and the most eloquent profanity was wasted on these heathen brutes. To make matters worse, the camels turned out to be more stubborn than mules. And as for looks—compared to a camel, a mule was a thing of beauty. Camels were dirty, smelly, noisy, uncouth and unpredictable. They would snort, spit, cough, and blow their noses at the most unexpected times and places. And if a soldier happened to stoop over to pick up something, his camel was very likely to take the opportunity to bite him. They would kick without warning—and in all directions at once. It didn't take long for the soldiers to come to hate them passionately. Only the few native camel drivers seemed to have any affection for these beasts.

But they were efficient. They could carry up to five hundred pounds of load—twice as much as a strong pack mule. And through normal terrain they could travel as much as thirty miles a day. And keep it up. No mule could do that, day in and day out. It was even said that a good dromedary could carry a man nearly one hundred miles a day on level ground. Here was speed the desert had never known before.

These good features, however, were eclipsed by some equally bad ones. Although they tried to use the proper kind of pack saddles on the camels, the soldiers could never acquire the knack of getting the load rigged so it would stay on. The packs kept slipping to the side or falling off. Also, in the mountains, the camels would get sore feet. Not having hoofs like the mules, their padded feet would tear and bleed on the sharp mountain rocks.

But on the other hand, these bad features were balanced against some good features discovered along the way. Not much food was needed for the animals. They could forage for themselves anywhere they stopped, and they would eat anything. The tough greasewood, the inedible mesquite, and the hostile cactus ears were all the same to camels—choice delicacies. And they could go without water for days. And to the surprise of everyone, at deep river crossings where mules were wont to balk, the stupid camels would plunge right in without any more urging than was normal.

The twenty-four camels in this first caravan traversed the 1,200 miles from Texas to California that hot summer with surprising speed and ease. Lieutenant Edward Fitzgerald Beale was in charge of this shake-down cruise, and he pronounced it a great success. His destination was Los Angeles. But he had no suitable place to keep them there, so he took them north to Fort Tejon. There they took up residence—Lieutenant Beale, the camels, the native drivers, and as many soldiers as could be persuaded to stay close to them. In 1860 another shipload of camels arrived in San Francisco and were taken south to Lieutenant Beale. But by this time they were becoming a liability.

In 1862, President Lincoln signed a bill authorizing a railroad to be built across the continent. This meant that there would be no further need for camels, at least on the long hauls across the desert, so Beale was confronted with the problem of disposing of them. He took them to Santa Barbara, and then up the coast to San Francisco, yet no one was particularly interested in camels. He shipped them across the Bay to Benecia, and there most of them were sold—some for zoos and circuses, some for private enterprise or speculation. So these Army camels that had received their basic training in Texas and Arizona were sold as war surplus in Benecia.

One buyer was a man named Samuel McLannigan, who planned to establish a freight line between California and Utah. He pastured some on a ranch in Sonoma, and some he took to Sacramento. In 1864, finding himself short of funds, McLannigan decided to put on a show. The State Fair was going on, and Mr. McLannigan advertised an exhibition of camels, climaxed by a race. He selected ten camels for the event. Among them was Old Tule, a thirty-five-year-old red camel of magnificent bearing. His native master, Haji Ali, had stayed with him all these years. Then there was Old Mary—and eight others, whose names and personalities have been forgotten.

A man named O.W. Dealing, whomever he was, got into the act also. Mr. Dealing's deal was, by some arrangement, to be the beneficiary of the gate receipts, and it was advertised that Mr. Dealing would ride one of the camels in this great race. Well, with a lot of ballyhoo and advertising, they got together a crowd of about a thousand people at the fairgrounds in Sacramento to watch the spectacle. When the time came, Mr. McLannigan got out on the racetrack to lead Old Tule around first just to acquaint him with the course and to see if the hike could be done. He got on his horse and led Old Tule with a rope; behind Old Tule came Mr. Dealing also riding a horse, and he busied himself applying the whip very vigorously to make Old Tule run. By dragging and pulling and pushing and whipping, they eventually got Old Tule around the track. He came up in front of the grandstand puffing and snorting and foaming, and the first lap was pronounced a success. Everybody applauded.

Next, the remainer of the camels were herded around the track as a kind of trial run. This was not easy. They ran, and they walked; they kicked and snorted, but they finally made the loop. And thus it was that the great moment arrived. Mr. Dealing was to ride one of the camels. He got up on Old Tule, with the other nine properly lined up. At the sound of the gun, off they went, snorting and whistling, spitting and braying for all they were worth. The dust flew and hoofs were flying in all directions. Around the track they went.

Mr. McLannigan, who was mounted on his horse, saw that disaster was riding in that race. Poor old Dealing up there on his saddle on one of those camels was tossing and pitching and bouncing and jouncing around like an erratic ball in a Bingo cage. When he got halfway around the track, Dealing was ready to jump overboard or fall or bounce off, so McLannigan spurred up his horse and caught up, stopped the race, and rescued poor old Dealing from his precarious hurricane deck.

Well, the race was a failure, but the gate receipts apparently were good—fifty cents from one-thousand people should have brought McLannigan $500, but when he counted the receipts he found that he had only $180. Somehow, somebody had put his hand in the till before the promoters themselves got to the money. So McLannigan was disappointed with his camel race in Sacramento. The next day he started north. He took his ten famous camels up along the Sacramento River, on the west side of the river along the freight route as far north as Red Bluff. They crossed the river there and headed eastward from Red Bluff toward Nevada. At this time camels were still attracting some attention as beasts of burden, and a group of businessmen in Downieville organized a camel transportation company to carry freight into Utah. But McLannigan and his camels went on over into Nevada. In the Washoe area they put the camels to work carrying coal to Virginia City and salt to various mines in the mining towns of Nevada. This was only a small number of the camels that had come to California; others had been shipped into Canada to work for the mines, but they had not proved successful and had been turned loose. These animals drifted down again into the deserts of Idaho and northern Utah.

You can imagine the consternation that would come into a mining camp when a caravan of camels came in loaded with freight. The horses would stampede with fright; they simply couldn't stand such a shocking spectacle. The mules that saw them, being smarter than horses, were first curious and then very suspicious, and they couldn't be managed for a while after being exposed to camels. And the people themselves, the old miners— some of them were frightened right out of their britches. It's been said that many an old drunk took the pledge after seeing what he couldn't believe when those camels came into town, right down the main street.

In Nevada, particularly, these camels became such a problem that in 1875 the Nevada Legislature passed a law prohibiting the use of camels on the highways of the state. So for the most part, the camels drifted. Turned loose, they roamed the deserts. And the native camel drivers drifted, too. One of them, the best known, whose name was Haiji Ali, got his name shortened by the Americans to Hi Jolly. He always wanted to become a miner, but he never quite made it. When the camels disappeared after their years of wandering, he took to driving mules and hauling freight.

What became of the camels? Rumor has it that they roamed the deserts and the Sierra Nevada mountains for many years afterward. Old prospectors reported seeing camels from time to time. One story is told about such a report. In a little mining town down in Arizona one night an old prospector came in, rushed up to the saloon, and ordered a drink. He could hardly believe what he had seen; he told about seeing a camel—a big red camel roaming out on the desert outside of town. All the boys in the saloon laughed at him and bought him another drink. They couldn't believe what he had seen—and neither could he. But when things quieted down, a dark old man crept up from one corner of the room and asked where he had seen this camel. The prospector told him. The old man disappeared. Up to then he had been unnoticed, except that he was an old foreign-looking fellow. Several days later, they found the old foreigner out on the desert lying dead with his arms locked around the neck of the big red camel that was also dead. Perhaps that was old Hi Jolly himself. There's a monument built for him in Arizona.

Legends continue to be told about the camels. Sometimes they are ghostly beasts roaming across the shifting desert sands wearing old leather Army saddles. Sometimes there's a ghostly skeleton strapped to the back of the phantom camel. Sometimes the story is of a crazed old miner who is leading three camels loaded with gold nuggets. Sometimes a phantom camel is seen far off in the distance crossing the sands like a ghostly ship with tattered sails. These camels don't exist now, but they did exist. And they left their ghosts to haunt the desert wastes of our West.

A Question of Marriage

In 1826 the sleepy little Spanish village of San Diego was beginning to awake to a new life. Trade with the rest of the world gave the old town a new burst of vigor, the dons of aristocratic and wealthy families like the Carrillos were looking for newer and more profitable enterprises than mere ranching, and the doñas of those same socially elite families were looking for more exciting and romantic gentlemen than the mere local boys. That's how it happened that San Diego was ready to welcome with open arms a certain young sea captain from Massachusetts who came sailing into the harbor in a handsome ship that had come the long journey around Cape Horn. His ancestry could be traced back to English nobility beginning at the time of the Norman Conquest, and his manners were dashing. The young man was just as eager to embrace San Diego as its citizens were to have him. He had indeed found his heaven, and the beautiful black-haired ladies were no less than angels. So it came to pass that Captain Henry Fitch became Don Enrique Fitch, and a señorita who was no less than Josefa Carrillo herself fell in love with him. She was the daughter of Don Joaquin Carrillo, and of her no greater thing than that could be said—except that she was sixteen then, and her beauty was breathtaking.

It was to be a love-match for these vibrant young people, and the Carrillo family nodded their heads in approval. All, that is, except Uncle Domingo Carrillo, who had a worry about it. Young Fitch was a foreigner. In those days true love could rise above nationality, but more serious was the fact that he was not a member of the Catholic faith. Even if the family agreed, no priest would be willing to perform the ceremony.

Fitch was not one to let the barrier of religion stand between him and the girl he would marry, and so on April 14, 1829, he was baptized at the Chapel of the Presidio in San Diego. A Dominican friar then agreed to perform the ceremony; so plans for the wedding went forward. It was to be a quiet family affair, set for late the next evening. But Uncle Domingo was still disturbed. The conversion of Fitch had been too easy; he was too eager and impetuous. Then there was still the question of his nationality. The Church frowned upon such a union as being unnatural and ill-advised. So at the last minute, almost when the ceremony was about to commence, Uncle Domingo refused to serve as a witness. This was a development in the state of affairs that terrified the poor friar, who had a dreadful vision of the most severe censure from his superiors for doing such a rash thing as offending Don Domingo by marrying these people. He quickly backed out, and there was no one to perform the ceremony. No amount of pleading or bribery could induce the unhappy friar to act. Perhaps if they went to another place, he believed that they might be married. Anywhere, just so it was outside his parish. If they wished, he might even go along and perform the ceremony for them—but not in San Diego, not in California. They might go to a foreign country and be united, and he wouldn't be held to blame for their rash misconduct.

There was a frantic family council. Some members departed with the priest. Others, like the young cousin Pio Pico, stayed around to help find a solution. There seemed to be no way out. Henry Fitch was beside himself with rage and frustration. Cousin

Pio Pico kept silent and tried to think, but no inspiration would come. Finally it was the young lady herself who solved the problem with a simple but daring question. "Don Enrique, why don't you just carry me off?" The boldness of it made her blush a little. But of course! Why not? She was nineteen now, old enough for any girl to know what she was doing. Pio Pico slapped his thigh in approval. Why hadn't he thought of it himself? Of course he would help. But the family mustn't be told. No point in taking any chances of another slip-up. The scheme was quickly worked out, and the next night Pio Pico took Josefa on horseback to a dark spot on San Diego Bay where Enrique and a boat were waiting, and they were off. Of all places, they were bound for Valparaiso, Chile.

On July 3, 1829, in Chile they were married by the Curate Orrego. Of course, word quickly got back to San Diego, and rumors spread. The gossips talked. The Church authorities were scandalized. The Carrillo family, shamed and outraged to all outward appearances, were secretly glad the affair had come off so well. After all, it wasn't so bad for a Spanish girl to marry an American. But of course the Church and the civil authorities had been defied, and until the local anger had cooled a little, perhaps the Fitches had better remain in South America.

They stayed away for one year. Then in 1830, Henry Fitch brought his wife back with an infant boy in her arms. Their ship docked, and they came ashore uncertain what their reception might be. They waited, and their worst fears were confirmed. No one from the family had come to meet them. Uncle Domingo was still offended, and her father could not endure the humiliation of acknowledging a willful and wayward daughter. The dignity of the whole Carrillo family was at stake. The whole village knew that the shame of this rash girl could not be endured, much less ever forgiven.

Alone the little Fitch family walked up the winding road to the great hacienda. A crowd had gathered, for the good people of San Diego knew that a crisis was a hand. They followed at a respectful distance, however, lest their whispers should betray their feelings. Old Carrillo would surely drive them away from his door.

The couple stopped at the gate. Josefa took the child from its father and held it close. The crowd waited in the background. Finally old Carrillo came out the door and stood in the shade of a large fig tree that spread over the path. He did not speak or beckon them to come. Silent and alone he stood, his white hair shining and his head held high and proud. The sadness of his face was all that revealed a breaking heart.

Josefa knelt by the gate. No one moved. Then, slowly with her child in her arms, she crawled on her knees up the walk toward her father. She held the baby out toward him, and the old man looked down at his grandson. With a sudden burst of tears in his eyes, the grandfather rushed forward and swept up the child and its mother into his arms. The little family of Fitch were welcome.

But there were other forces to be reckoned with. It was not long before Henry Fitch was served with an ultimatum. Padre Sanchez of San Gabriel, the ecclesiastical judge of the territory, summoned Fitch and his wife to present themselves to answer to serious charges. They were not legally married in the eyes of the Church.

In response, Fitch sent his marriage certificate to Father Sanchez, and then sailed up the coast to Santa Barbara and Monterey. But the ecclesiastical law of California reached with a long arm. An order was sent to Monterey for the arrest of Fitch and for the removal of the lady Doña Josefa, who was to be "deposited" in some respectable home. The Carrillo family closed ranks to protect their beloved Josefa. She went to stay with Captain Cooper, whose wife was a sister to General Mariano Vallejo. And Vallejo had married a Carrillo—Francesca Benicia Carrillo, sister of Josefa Fitch. Henry Fitch was taken to San Gabriel, where he was held prisoner in one of the rooms of the Mission. His wife was allowed to go to San Gabriel to visit him, and there was much questioning of all persons having knowledge of the affair.

All the influence that the great families of California could muster—the Carrillos, the Vallejos, the Perez family, Pio Pico (who later became governor)—all stood by their Josefa. Finally, on December 28, the decision was given that the marriage was not to be annulled. The wife was given back to her husband, and the two were ordered to church the next Sunday to take the sacraments that should have preceded the marriage.

But the judgment of Vicar Sanchez went further. It said: "Yet, considering the great scandal which Don Enrique has caused in this province, I condemn him to give as penance and reparation a bell of at least fifty pounds in weight for the Church of Los Angeles. Moreover, the couple must present themselves in Church with lighted candles in their hands to hear high mass for three Días Festivos and recite together for thirty days one-third of the Rosary of the Holy Virgin." There is no doubt that Don Enrique, like a good churchman, did penance—until he got to the matter of the bell. For it is of record that long after the couple left southern California and settled in Sonoma, the Church at Los Angeles was still without a bell.

The brother-in-law, General Vallejo, advised Fitch to come north, live in Sonoma near him, and apply for a land grant in the area. This was done, and by 1840 Fitch had selected a man named Cyrus Alexander to manage his vast Rancho Sotoyome, which was near where the town of Healdsburg now stands. The ranch prospered, and so did the Fitch family. By 1848 they had several children, and it was decided that they should settle on the Sotoyome ranch and make it their home.

But fate seemed determined once again to come between Henry Fitch and his wife. Or perhaps it was his enemies who were becoming too numerous. He had many enterprises, including a land grant in San Francisco which he shared with several other men, and conflicting interests were at stake. According to family records these partners were unscrupulous men who wanted to get rid of Fitch. At Christmas time, 1848, he was called to San Francisco for a business meeting and banquet. This was a bad time to be away from his family, to whom he was totally devoted, but the message seemed urgent. Josefa had a premonition that something might go wrong, but a wife could not stand in the way of important business matters. He promised to return as soon as possible, and it was agreed that just this once Christmas could be postponed for a few days, and to satisfy the children he hinted that he might bring something special from the big stores in the city. The goodbyes were sadder than usual when Henry Fitch left his family.

In San Francisco the business meeting was unpleasant. The banquet which followed it, however, was exceptionally festive and gay. Many of the leading citizens were there, and so were his partners. His distrust of them had increased, but for some inexplicable reason these treacherous men were surprisingly cordial. They even insisted on pouring some special wine that they had brought for the occasion.

Before the banquet was over, Fitch became deathly sick. His partners offered to take him to his hotel, but he lost consciousness before he could get there. When he awoke he learned that he was on a ship bound for San Diego. He was still in great pain. Sensing the seriousness of his condition he asked for the captain, and in the presence of witnesses he made his last will and testament. To a good friend who was looking after him on shipboard he left his gold watch. Other trusted friends were released from their debts to him, and his estates were left to his wife and children. He died in San Diego on January 14, 1849. Fate had won, and Josefa Carrillo was a widow.

She moved to the adobe house that Henry had built for her on the Sotoyome Rancho, and there she remained for the rest of her life. For forty-four years she lived in seclusion. And when she died at the age of 83 she was buried in Healdsburg. Her family grew up there, and some of the property is still in the hands of people who are descendants of this romantic couple from an age that has long since passed into history.

The family proudly remembers that they clung fast to each other in spite of insurmountable obstacles and proved that their love was true. Yet perhaps the unkindest irony in their story is the fact that fate won against them after all. For Henry Fitch lies buried in San Diego, separated by hundreds of miles from his wife, whose final resting place is in the town where they had planned to grow old together.

How to Dissolve a Partnership

THE PROPERTY SETTLEMENT may not have been unique in the history of separations, but considering the place and time—the town of Freestone, California, in the 1840s—it was certainly unusual. Sonoma County history is a bit sketchy on the matter, since historians are bound to the recorded facts. But as a folklorist I had long suspected that there was more to the story than met the ear, a matter on which the folk of later generations would have their own versions surviving in oral tradition. I reasoned that such a temperamental division of property, when a long and prosperous relationship finally broke up, must have some special human angle, and this was the story I wanted to collect.

My antiquarian informant, who purportedly knew what the folk remembered, was willing enough to tell it but only after he had had his fun with me, as many old-timers do who have a good story to tell; he delayed the narrative with diversionary yarns to heighten the suspense.

"So you want to hear the story about how old Dawson and McIntosh dissolved their partnership. Right here in the town of Freestone, it was. That was over a hundred years ago—more than that, I guess—so it was just a little before my time here. But I heard it plenty of times, though. Sure was comical.

"Puts me in mind of the time when me and old Elmer Yancey dissolved our partnership, as you might call it. Yeah. We was partners, him and me, in a lot of things back in them days—that was long before your time. Elmer, he was a high-stepper and a fancy kind of a feller, always lookin' to get one on the next sucker that come along, you know. He was as slick as two shoats in the axle grease. He even tried to put one over on me, but I got him in the end. Yeah.

"Him and me, we was livin' together in a little shack there at Bodega, just over the hill, there, and we bought a cow together. She was a right good milker, too. And old Elmer, he says, 'Accordin' to the laws of legal corporate ownership, we're supposed to agree on how we want to divide things up, was we ever to want to. So I guess we've got to divvy up this here cow. Suppose you take the front end, and I'll take the hind end—just to keep her straight. And you'll notice,' says he, 'that I'm gettin' the dirty end of the deal.'

"So we done it that way.

Then it was, I discovered what he'd done to me. Come to find out, I had to feed my end of that cow, and all he had to do was milk his'n. I was payin' out and he was takin' in the profits and laughing his fool head off over it.

"But I got even. I decided to dissolve our partnership. So come fall, I went out one day and I just butchered my end of that cow—and his end died. Yeah! That asset of his shore collapsed right there."

The old-timer chuckled over his joke, which was an old wheeze that I had heard many times. That wasn't exactly the partnership that I had come to Freestone to hear about, but I figured he'd get to the right story in his own sweet time. What I wanted was the story of the two old pioneers who had owned a house jointly in Freestone back in 1837, and what they did about it when they had an argument and decided to break up their partnership.

"Sure, I heard about McIntosh and Dawson," the old man said.

"Or was it Black and Dawson? Anyway, they weren't the only ones that dissolved their community property over here. One time there was two loggers who worked in the woods for a sawmill that was at Bodega Corners. You know, the first owner of this country from redwoods around there in them days, too. And, so they say, there was several big sawmills around there. Anyhow, these two fellers was workin' in the woods. I don't remember that I ever heard their names, but they were workin' in the woods as partners.

"It seems they lived together in a shanty that they owned jointly, as you might say. Well, one day they got mad at each other over something. In them days, you know, them loggers would fight at the drop of a hat. And hats was mighty loose. Anyway, it seems that they was out in the woods, and they got into some kind of a ruckus and had a fight. So they decided right then and there to dissolve their joint assets. One of 'em got so mad he went back to their shanty to figure out what to do to get even. Seems like they had their shanty divided—one had one side and the other had the other side. Anyway, this feller, he went over to the other feller's side, and he set her afire. Then he come back to the woods, and he says to the first feller, 'In case you might be interested, your half of the house is on fire.' And the first feller, he just sat down, and he was so mad he just says, 'Hell, let' 'er burn, and see if I care.' So she burned right down, and both fellers lost out. Now, ain't that a corker?"

But this was not the story I wanted, either. The old man was, however, getting closer, and eventually he gave me his version of the McIntosh and Dawson affair.

The Rancho Bodega, which the Mexican government granted to Captain Stephen Smith, extended originally from Jenner at the mouth of the Russian River, down the coast to Bodega Bay, and inland as far as the Smith mansion near Bodega Corners about four miles inland from the coast. When Smith died his widow married a man named Tyler Curtis. But by this time, in the 1850s, the vast property was plagued with squatters. Smith had tolerated them, but Curtis was more businesslike and tried to expel them. Failing in this, he agreed to sell to the squatters at very low prices, and the issue was finally settled. Similar problems were faced by other owners of large Mexican land grants during the same period. Perhaps the best known of these was John Sutter, who lost most of his vast holdings to squatters and never did collect for the property which, under the law, was his.

To the east of Smith's grant lay other ranches that had been given to enterprising Americans by various Mexican governors. Among these was the Rancho Estero Americano. It was originally held jointly by Edward McIntosh, a recently transplanted Scotsman, and James Dawson, an American. The ranch bordered on what is now the little town of Freestone, which lies in a fertile valley between Sebastopol and Bodega.

In the 1830s and early '40s, when most large grants were made, it was necessary for the owner to be a Mexican citizen. To hold their land, therefore, such men as John Sutter and Stephen Smith had become Mexicans. Edward McIntosh had become a naturalized American, but when he reached California and realized what could be gained in terms of a large grant of land, he was willing to change nationality again and become a Mexican citizen. But Dawson, on the other hand, was not of a mind to give up his American citizenship so readily. And this was how the trouble started.

McIntosh urged Dawson to take Mexican citizenship, but the more he argued the more stubborn Dawson became. "No, I think we should wait," he reasoned. "I think if we can just hang on to it long enough, all this land will come into the United States, anyway. And I don't fancy the idea of becomin' no Mexican."

"Are you daft, man?" McIntosh argued. "All you have to do is sign the papers. Then the land will be ours for keeps, and we can go about our business workin' it with the cattle and all the rest. You'll be ahead in the end, and no harm to our conscience."

But Dawson refused. So McIntosh secretly went ahead and recorded the grant in his own name as a Mexican citizen, and he became the sole legal owner of the ranch. The two men had built a fairly respectable house on the place. They had traded for good lumber from the mill at Bodega and had built well. The house had both strength and beauty. They were proud of their home, and in it they had been living happily for five years when the crisis came.

Dawson was well aware of the rule of the Mexican governor to give land only to Mexican citizens. He was also acutely conscious of the fact that his partner had tried to persuade him to make the necessary move. But he couldn't shake the feeling that no one had the right to force him to give up his nationality just because of a technicality. It was clear that he was losing his property, and in his anger he turned against the man who was taking it, his partner. The more Dawson thought about it the sorrier he felt for himself and the more he blamed McIntosh. At last it was decided that the partnership between them would have to be dissolved.

"Ye've no right to the land, and that through your own foolishness," said McIntosh. "And there's nothin' you can do about it."

"What's mine's mine," yelled Dawson. "And by Jupiter I'm goin' to have it!" And he brought his fist down on the table so hard the empty whiskey glasses jumped a little. "You can keep the land, if you are so dad-blasted greedy for it. But everything else goes fifty-fifty."

"Well, that seems fair—if it can be done," said McIntosh. "Now as for the cattle—"

"Fifty-fifty!" said Dawson. "I'll take my half; you keep yours."

"And the other livestock?"

"Fifty-fifty, right down the middle."

"And that pile of logs we've got ready for the mill?"

"Right down the middle."

"And what about this house?"

"Right down the middle!" exclaimed Dawson, and he smote the table another mighty blow.

"As ye say," said McIntosh. And that was the end of the discussion. The next day the great division of their assets began. The cattle, horses, pigs, and even the chickens were divided evenly, and Dawson's share was taken to some unclaimed land to the northeast about half a mile. It happened that at first count the chickens didn't divide evenly, so the odd hen was killed and eaten by both men as sustenance for the day; and thus even she contributed to each—right down the middle. All the movable assets were scrupulously divided.

There remained only the beautiful house which both had shared equally. "The house stays with the land," said McIntosh.

"Fifty-fifty, right down the middle," said Dawson. He went out to his wagon and got his mighty cross-cut saw, and forthwith he began to saw the house exactly in two. Solomon could not have done it better. McIntosh watched in horror. But a bargain was a bargain—right down the middle.

When the house was sawed in two, Dawson—with some hired help he picked up—got skids under his half. He hitched four horses to the skids and began to drag his half of the house away. The operation took several days, and the congregated onlookers wondered whether the bisected remnants could stand the shock of the operation. But the men had built well; the two halves stood, each with its open wound exposed to the world.

Dawson dragged his half up Salmon Creek to a point where it makes its bend at the town of Freestone, and there he brought her to rest. Each man then patched up the gaping side of his half, and life went on. It is said that both halves of that house are still in use today, though of course with modern improvements they are not recognizable now.

Dawson later did become a Mexican citizen after all—when he married a Mexican girl, the popular Maria Antonia Caseres, the eldest daughter of the man who at one time was the only white resident of Yerba Buena. And then Dawson received a grant of his own—the Rancho Cañada de Poggolimi. And the folk say he lived happily ever after.

Captain Jack

I CAN LOOK THROUGH the bars out toward Fort Klamath and see that sunset will soon come. Behind me in the prison cell where I stand the shadows are cold and dark. Outside the window they are building a gallows for hanging me. My name is Captain Jack. I am Modoc. People have been afraid of me and hated me, and the white man has hunted me. It is all over now. I look down at the heavy irons locked to my legs, and I think back to a time when it all started.

In the white man's year of 1852 I was a young man. I lived with my father, chief of the Modocs, lived north of Tule Lake on Lost River. My father and I lived at peace with the white man. Then I did the things a Modoc boy should do. I learned to hunt and fish. I learned the dances and the ceremonial songs, and the song to greet the rising sun, the song for night when the end of day comes, the song for dying. We sang the songs of the old days. We respected the ways of our fathers. I learned to be part of all living things, and the animals were my spirit brothers, and the birds, and the trees. If we killed a deer or rabbit for food, we told them why we had to do it so they would understand. And we learned to talk to the trees and thank them for giving us their wood, and the willows and tules for giving us the things we needed. And we never killed anything, only when we had to, for our spirits were all one. That's how I lived with my father.

But the time comes when some Shasta Indians, no friends of ours, attack a white man wagon train. Kill most of the settlers coming in. Just a few get away. Then ranchers and miners nearby want to get revenge. Come out hunting for Indians. All kinds of Indians will do. No matter who—kill 'em. They come to my village and attack us—shoot, kill men, kill women, kill children. I can hear babies cry, women cry.

So my father calls a council of war. The wise men sit there, and they say, "White men kill you; you kill them." My name then is Kientpoos, son of the chief. This talk makes trouble in my heart, so I speak. Old men listen. I say, "I am Modoc. Not afraid of white man. But we be wrong to kill them. They kill our people for thing other Indians do. Too many white men; can't kill 'em all. More will come. Pretty soon all Modocs get killed. All dead. I say make peace with white man." When I am through speaking, old men laugh. Say, "Some day you be chief of Modocs, but you talk like woman. You talk peace. Can be no peace." Council over. I go to sleep. Worry about it.

In few days something happen. Wagon train comes through. My father and other braves attack the wagon train. Kill all the whites but a few, maybe, escape to Yreka. Over there, Yreka, is old Indian fighter, name of Ben Wright. He get men together, go out hunting. Want to kill Indian. Come looking for my people. They bring with them a bad medicine called strychnine. Come to my village, all the same in peace. Say they want to talk with Modoc brothers. They have big feast and ask for a council. Old Schonchin says, "Don't eat the white man's meat. Not good for Modocs." But I come to feast and sit. Listen to talk. The Indians don't eat the meat, and white men don't eat the meat. Then Ben Wright knows something wrong. Take out his gun and shoot man sitting by him. That man is my father. Then all white men take out guns, shoot

Indians sitting next to them. Kill forty-one braves of my tribe. I and some others run away to the lava beds and hide.

Now, who is to be chief? Schonchin John and others say they want war. He would like to be the leader. The people talk about it. I say better to live in peace with white men. But Schonchin John and others say they want war.

I want to learn about white man and his way. Go over to Yreka. In Yreka is man named Elisha Steele. He names me Captain Jack from a good man he knows. I like name; keep it rest of my life. Mr. Steele comes, calls tribe together for big talk. People make me chief. Mr. Steele help make treaty. Decide where tribe's lands should be. My home is to be on Lost River. That is country that I love.

But by 1864 many, many white men come; want my people's land. Government says, "You, all Modocs, move to reservation. Give 'em land." We want peace. So we go to reservation. No good. So my people slip away, come back home. In 1869 Mr. Meacham is new Indian Superintendent. He comes to talk us into going to a reservation up north where Klamath are. He makes promise that everything be all right, but I think about Ben Wright and my father. Schonchin John and Curly Head Doctor say, "Kill Meacham now. That's only way to settle this thing." But instead, I sign paper. Then they put my people into wagons; we go way north to Klamath reservation. The Klamath are old enemies of Modoc. Hate each other. Afraid to live together.

Now it is winter time. Cold. My women and children are cold; have no clothes. We live on fish and roots we can dig. But when we go out to fish, Klamath say, "They are our fish. We let you fish in our streams, but you must give us some." We tell Indian agent, but he just laugh at us. In the spring our men go out and cut logs to build houses. Cut lots of logs. But one morning we find logs all stolen. Klamath say, "You can cut logs, but you got to give us some." We tell officer in charge, but he says, "If you Modocs cause us any more trouble, you have to move to another place further away."

So one night we slip away. We go back home on Lost River. But our land is already taken by white man. We have friends in Yreka, ranchers who are good to us. John Fairchild and Press Dorris are friends to Indians. But then come soldiers with Ivan Applegate and Oliver Applegate to talk peace. They tell us, "Go back to reservation." But we are tired of talk. We say, "We no want to kill white man. We no want your dead bodies. We want our Lost River country back again. You give it to us or we kill you. We are not afraid to die. We can't live with Klamath; they have been enemies of our people from times no one can remember. There is a stone wall from earth to sky between us. Leave us alone. We are tired of talk, talk, all the time talk."

They promise us a reservation on Lost River. But we never get it. Some Modocs steal horses from settlers. This is bad. But I can't stop them. In 1872 soldiers come again. They say, "You go to reservation with Klamath or we kill you." I think maybe this is better than fighting. But Scarface Charley won't give up his gun. A soldier tries to take it away from him. Calls him dog. So Scarface Charley shoots. Then shooting starts all over the village and in Hooker Jim's village across the river. Our people slip away through the sagebrush and hide in lava beds. Indians are very angry now, and kill many ranchers. They even kill some men who are good to us. But I can't stop it. Now we know white men will come back to kill us, so we go to caves in the lava beds. We put food there, hide it in many places.

Next year, 1873, come soldiers again. Four hundred white men to fight our fifty. They camp by the lava beds and talk about the scalps they are going to take next day. I want to stop it, but don't know how. Scarface Charley, Hooker Jim, Schonchin John, and Curly Head Doctor all say, "We must kill them all now." Curly Head Doctor says, "I'll make strong medicine. We win tomorrow."

So next day, soldiers start into lava beds to kill us. Then a big fog comes in. Heavy fog. They can't see, and fall on sharp rocks. We are hiding in cracks and behind rocks to shoot them. Soldiers are afraid because they can't see soldiers lost in fog. Our Indians shoot soldiers, but they can't see us. All day like this. Soldiers are afraid, and that night they go back to camp. They have sixteen dead and many wounded—all white men. No Indian hurt. We say, "Curly Head Doctor's medicine was good."

Then comes General Canby. He brings men, maybe two thousand. He set up a tent for peace talk. Interpreter is Winema. She is married to Riddle, a white man. She is translator for talk about peace. But too late for talk of peace.

Now it is the time of the early flowers. Indians say, "Kill the peace commissioners. Ask them to come, leave guns behind. You shoot General Canby; we shoot all others." They say, "You remember Ben Wright." I don't want to do it. But somebody throws a woman's shawl at me; yells, "You are a woman—not fit to lead Modocs."

So we tell peace commissioners, "Come to tent. Leave guns behind." Winema tells commissioners, "Look out!" But General Canby says it's all right. Everybody comes to the peace tent. Lots of talk, but we don't listen. Then somebody makes a signal, and I shoot General Canby.   Another commissioner is killed, too. Meacham gets shot, falls down, is half scalped. He looks like dead. Winema and Riddle run away. Then I put on General Canby's coat. This is good medicine.

In a few days more soldiers come. They bring big guns called mortars that shoot over head and the bullets fall down on us. Then soldiers come to close in around us in a circle. They come, look in cave, but we are gone. We go to another place in lava beds. This happen many times. We always get away. But pretty soon we get tired, hungry. Children cry, for many times is no food or water. Not many bullets left. Women say better to get shot than starve. The children are cold, hungry, sick.

Soldiers catch most of my people, one or two at a time. I get away every time. Hooker Jim and Bogus Charley go over to soldiers. Say they will help hunt Indians for money. Soldiers follow us from one cave to another. Dig us out like coyotes from den. Pretty soon we can't go on no more. Tired, hungry, no more bullets; we got to give up. I say, "Now it is the time. Jack's legs give out. I am ready to die."

Then soldiers take me to Fort Klamath; hold me to talk to council for my life. No need for council. No man to talk for me. My own people join soldiers and speak things against me. Pretty soon the judge say, "Captain Jack, what you got to say?" I don't tell 'em in English, but talk Modoc, so Winema comes. She can be interpreter. I have irons on my legs, on my hands, but I stand up to speak. She tells my words in the white man's words, and the white man writes down what I say:

"When I was boy, I had it in my heart to be a friend to white man. I was their friend until my own people turned my heart. They forced me to kill General Canby. You white men did not conquer me. My own braves conquered me. Some of them are here today, free men; I am in irons. They are the ones who wanted to kill the peace-mans. I fought against it. But they threw the woman's blanket before me, and I said yes. If I had known they would turn against me, you would not have me here today with chains on my legs and smiles on your faces. . . .

"You say I am bad man. You say I killed Canby. Yes, I did kill him, but I see no crime in my heart. My heart is not bad. The ones most guilty are the ones now free. If white man's law would not be crooked like the snake, they would be here in chains with me and these others.

"I am ashamed to die with rope around my neck. I wanted to die on battlefield with gun in my hand. But I am not afraid. I think of my people and hope you don't treat them bad on my account. . . .

"Now here I am. . . killed one man, after I had been fooled by him many times, and forced to do it by my own warriors. The law says hang him. He is nothing but an Indian, anyhow. Let me hang, then. I am not afraid to die. I will show you how a Modoc can die. I am done."

These words I said. Now I look out the window and wait for tomorrow, but in my heart there is no song for the rising sun. Scaffold will be ready tomorrow.

Dorsey the Mailman

"YOU CAN'T TELL ME that dogs ain't as smart as people. I've even seen a few that was a lot smarter than some human jackasses I could mention; and when it comes to being honest or dependable, well I've had dealings with a lot of cusses that couldn't hold a candle to a good dog." So spoke my aging friend Ace Morgan as we sat in the shade of my patio one hot summer day and talked of ships and shoes and sealing wax, and cabbages and kings.

The dog that evoked this particular pearl of wisdom was a handsome Irish setter that we called Sam. Actually, he was not our dog; his owner was a neighbor who lived three houses away, a captain of a Pan Am Boeing 747 that flew between San Francisco and Tokyo. But when his master was away Sam lived with us. My wife fed him and kept him relatively free from fleas and even taught him a few words. In fact, Sam had a pretty good vocabulary. And both our place and his owner's became his territory to protect from canine invaders, and on command he would trot back and forth from one sphere of responsibility to the other.

This daily ritual of Sam's gained him Ace Morgan's respect and placed him in a category somewhat above that attainable by most of the human species. "Yes, sir, you're smart and good lookin' both," and Ace reached down to scratch that worthy canine behind the ears. Sam acknowledged the compliment with a thump of the tail without bothering to alter his comfortable position, which was with the rear end lying in sprawling relaxation and the front resting on the chest with head erect and paws crossed in serene dignity.

This attention to Sam seemed to stir up old memories in Ace. I could see he felt a story coming on. He filled his pipe, sat for a moment in deep thought, and then began his narrative.

"Speaking of smart, Sam here puts me in mind of a dog I heard of once that ought to get into the history books. Maybe he is, for all I know. I picked up this story when I was down there in the Mojave Desert doing a little prospecting, and a feller told me about this dog. That was years ago, but everybody knew about this particular dog, and by then he'd been dead of old age a good many years, and his pups dead of old age, too. The feller told me it was way back in the 1880s when all this happened, and I guess that's about right.

"This dog's name was Dorsey, and some said he was a big shepherd and others said he was a collie. I guess that doesn't matter too much. I'd go for the shepherd, myself, though.

"Well, anyway, it was down in the old town of Calico, way out in the Mojave Desert. It's a ghost town now, but back in them days it was a pretty lively little mining camp. And about three miles away, over in Odessa Canyon, there was Bismarck where they had the Garfield, the Odessa, and the Occidental mines. Some called it East Calico, but it was really Bismarck.

"There was a post office in Calico, and a feller named Jim Stacy ran it along with a general store he had there; and his partner—a brother, the way I heard it—also had a store up at Bismarck.

"Well, one night this dog showed up at Stacy's store. He was pretty bedraggled, footsore, and hungry, so Stacy took him in. He fed him up to a pretty good shape, and they got to be close friends, him and that dog. Well, every few days Stacy's brother would come down from Bismarck for the mail and other business, and so the dog got to be good friends with him, too. A feller named Dorsey had a kind of a bob-tailed contract to carry the mail between Calico and Bismarck, but he flattened out on it and one day he just disappeared, so Stacy's brother had to take the mail back and forth for the miners. But he wasn't none too regular.

"Anyhow, one day the dog followed the brother back to Bismarck, and he made that a kind of second home. If he got tired of one place he'd just trot off to the other. So he got to thinking he owned both places.

"One day Stacy had a need to send an urgent message to his brother up at the mine, but he couldn't get away himself and there was nobody else around. There lay the dog in the shade by the front door. Stacy looked at him, and the dog cocked one eye up at Stacy. Says Stacy, 'Mr. Dog, I think you might just do for this job. It's about time you started to earn your keep. How about it?' And the dog just flapped his tail on the porch boards a time or two as if to say, 'Well, boss, I just might be talked into doing you a good turn now and then if the pay is right.'

"So Stacy fixed up a kind of a collar around his neck and tied his note to it. Then says he, 'Now you git! Off to Bismarck with you!' Stacy waved his arm in the proper direction and the dog started off. He stopped a time or two to look back, just to make sure that he had the right signal, and Stacy waved his arm again. So off he went and disappeared up the road.

"In about an hour here came the dog back. And he had an answer to the note tied to him. Stacy fed him a nice piece of meat for a reward, and then he began to study on the matter. Says he, 'I do believe you'd make a better mailman than Dorsey ever was.' So he made the dog a nice leather collar, and he named him Dorsey.

"The next day, at about the same time, Stacy wrote another note to his brother and he put a real honest-to-God letter with it, tied it to Dorsey's collar, and sent him off again. In about an hour, here he was back with an answer and a real letter to mail out.

"And that's how it started that Dorsey became the mailman. Every day Stacy would fasten a little bundle of mail to Dorsey's collar and send him off, and just as regular as clockwork here he would come back with a bundle of return mail. They made a little sack and fixed it to a harness like a pack saddle, and in sandstorm or hot weather the mail always went through. Dorsey seemed to like his job, and he always got the right amount of appreciation after every trip.

"This went on for three or four years, winter and summer. Even when people went back and forth they only carried the heavy stuff; they always let Dorsey carry his load of first class letters. He took pride in his work and would never let anything interfere while he was on duty. Sometimes a person on the road would try to stop him, but he would always circle wide around and keep on going.

"He got to be pretty famous in that country. Once I even saw a picture they took of him that showed him with his front feet up on a box and the mail sack strapped to his back. He got to be a kind of a celebrity, and on Christmas you can bet your bottom dollar he was generously remembered.

"But sometimes being a hero doesn't last very long. After awhile the mines shut down. Bismarck closed out and before long Calico was just a ghost town. The Stacys had to pull out, and of course they took Dorsey with them. They went on a visit to San Francisco, and the news got out about Dorsey, and the newspapers ran stories on him. So when he got his name in the paper he was a hero again, but that didn't last long, either.

"Stacy gave him to a friend in San Francisco, but Dorsey didn't seem to like city life. He was always looking for a way to get back to Calico, and that's how it happened that somebody stole him. His new owners offered a reward of a hundred dollars to anyone who would return him, but nobody ever claimed the reward.

"Finally, after a few days, Dorsey came back to his San Francisco home. Through his own intelligence and dog sense he had managed to get away from whoever had stolen him, and I guess he decided that having a good home in the city was not so bad after all. So he settled down to a good retirement and gave up his dream of ever getting back to the desert and the good old days. But if every dog has his day, you might say that old Dorsey sure had his."

The Mystery of Murieta's Head

IT WAS NOT EXACTLY a quest for the Holy Grail. In fact, there was nothing holy about it. On the contrary, the elusive object might be considered a symbol of evil, a grisly relic of man's greed and inhumanity. I wanted to find it, not to fulfill any compelling need, but merely to satisfy a recurring curiosity. The object of this fascination was the long lost head of the legendary California bandit, Joaquin Murieta.

The gruesome trophy, if it ever had existed at all, was supposed to have been lost in the San Francisco earthquake and fire of 1906. There had indeed been a human head on exhibition in one place or another for decades before that catastrophe, and I had seen a poster advertising the display for those who wanted to pay one dollar for the thrill of viewing it preserved in its large jar.

Some people said the so-called head was a fake. Historians claimed that the legend of Murieta was mostly romantic fiction based on the fact that there was a bandit called Joaquin who was killed by a posse and decapitated, but the head was finally lost. The rumor persisted, however, that the head had not been destroyed and that somewhere it lay hidden. It was even hinted that the vengeful ghost of Joaquin still haunted California, and that the earthquakes, fires, and floods would continue until the lost head was restored to its body.

Whether true or not, the romantic story of Joaquin Murieta has survived and grown to become California's most popular legend. Among Mexican families the bandit is remembered and revered as a Robin Hood. As late as 1980 a Mexican woman in Sacramento said, "Yes, the story is alive. Each and every one of us has his own version, and it means the same to us like you have your George Washington."

The story began in 1851. In a little cabin on the Stanislaus River in Central California lived a young Mexican. He was a very handsome and intelligent man, apparently of a good family, who with his brother had come up from Sonora, Mexico, to farm and perhaps pan a little gold in this new land of El Dorado. He brought with him his lovely young bride, Rosita, or perhaps her name was Carmelita; the stories differ, and no one is quite sure.

Together, in that little cabin by the river, they lived through a quiet, happy summer. They took a little gold from the stream, and they talked about how they would plant some corn when spring came. They knew nothing of the Californian's laws, and when it was explained to them that it was illegal for Mexicans to own mining claims or take gold from the California rivers, they merely shrugged and went on with their work. God had put the gold there. It belonged to everybody. And they took only the little that fortune put into their hands to pay for their work.

Such flagrant disregard for the God-given rights of the master race outraged the American miners, who vowed that such lawlessness must not go unpunished. One night a small group of bully boys from town, drunk on liquor and fired with hatred, burst into the cabin by the river. Angry words and threats quickly exploded into a fight. When Joaquin's brother reached for his gun he was shot down. Joaquin fought like a mad man, but there were too many against him. Squirming and cursing, he was held to watch while his beautiful wife—innocent, frightened, and helpless—was brutally attacked and then murdered. Then he was dragged out to a post in the yard. He was stripped to the waist and with his arms behind him he was tied to a post so he could face his punishment. With a horsewhip they lashed him until the blood came. As he stood there straining at the ropes, each time the leather whip cut across his bare chest and shoulders he swore an awful vengeance. He memorized the ugly faces of his attackers and swore that he would kill them every one. Then he slumped into unconsciousness, and his assailants left him for dead.

The next day, when sober people found the place, Joaquin was gone. It was whispered that he had drifted north somewhere, but no one knows for sure where he went. The marks of the whip gradually healed, but the memory of his pain and the hatred for his enemies seemed to grow stronger. The next time he appeared it was as a bandit. He had gathered around him a band of other Mexicans who had grievances, or who wanted a quick profit and were not afraid to kill for it. The handsome young Mexican soon became the respected and feared leader of bold and ruthless outlaws. Always splendidly dressed, he rode at the head of his band on a magnificent horse, and his very name struck fear to any who might stand in his way. The men who had killed his wife and brother one by one disappeared or were found dead in dark and lonely places, and everyone knew whose vengeance had overtaken them.

To his foes he was a cruel and deadly enemy, but to his friends he was a heroic benefactor. He was never known to turn down a friend who needed relief from oppression. Many poor Mexicans received his generous help, and they thanked him and asked the saints to bless and protect him. Whenever he needed a place to hide, they sheltered him and kept his secrets. He had become their Robin Hood.

In 1851 he and his gang settled about three miles north of Marysville. They stole horses, robbed immigrant wagons, held up stage coaches, and killed whoever got in their way or were so foolish as to try to capture them. The vigilantes organized a large force to hunt him down, so Joaquin quietly slipped away and went further north and wintered near Mount Shasta. After that, he was always on the move. At San Jose a posse almost cornered him, but he got away. Some say he went to Carmel, and it was there that a priest painted his picture.

Such a picture did exist. Perhaps it was painted by a priest. It showed a man supposed to be named Joaquin, with wild eyes, a fierce moustache, and a cruel face. Other artists later copied this picture, and in each successive portrait the outlaw became more dashing, more handsome, more gallant, and his costume became more colorful and splendid. These pictures only reflect the growing legend.

There is a telling of how a cattle buyer was camped by a little stream one night as he was driving his cattle to market in one of the San Joaquin Valley towns. Five young Mexicans rode into his camp just at dusk and asked for some supper. He obligingly gave them food, and they spread out their bedrolls and slept by his camp that night. The next morning, when they awoke, he was cooking breakfast for them.

"Well, how is Señor Joaquin this morning?" he asked.

The young leader looked startled and suddenly became tense. One of his companions drew his gun, looked a long time at the cattle man, and then grinned. "So you theenk you know heem?"

"Yes, I knew him the minute he rode in last night," said the cattle man. The Mexican then asked why the driver hadn't killed him last night when he was asleep to collect the reward.

"Why, that's easy, friend. I don't like to kill men. And I don't want the reward. Besides, you fellers never did me any harm. If every man that deserved to hang went supperless, there'd be empty chairs at more tables than mine," said the cattle man. Joaquin smiled and promised the man that he would never be sorry. And the people say that from that day on, this man never lost a head of cattle to any Mexican bandits.

The reward for the outlaw grew. It attracted many adventurers, some of whom gave their lives to the vengeance of Joaquin. With increasing interest and satisfaction he read the reward notices. One beautiful Sunday morning in Stockton, while the bells were ringing for church and the fine ladies and gentlemen were walking to worship, a handsome young Mexican came riding along the street on a beautiful black horse. He was wearing a fashionable sombrero, flashing buckles, and spurs of silver. He stopped here and there to look in the shop windows. The young ladies cast admiring glances his way and thought, "What a rich young man he must be."

He rode over to the side of the building where some posters had been na led to the wall. One of the posters read: "Reward: $5,000 for the bandit Joaquin." The stranger got off his horse, took a pencil out of his pocket and wrote something over the poster. Then he remounted his horse and rode away. The ladies and gentlemen rushed up to look at the poster to see what he had written. On the reward notice he had crossed out the $5,000 and had written under it, "I will give $10,000," and it was signed, "Joaquin."

This episode has been repeated many times. One woman reported that her grandparents saw it happen. They had gone to Stockton to trade and when they came into the town they saw that the people were very excited and they were standing in front of a bulletin board, and milling around and talking, and they wondered what was the matter. Upon coming closer, they found that attentions had focused on a reward notice posted for the head of Joaquin Murieta. "They saw a young man on horseback at the edge of the crowd, sitting very quietly on his horse and watching the crowd." Finally, the story continued, "He yelled a real loud yell and pulled his pistol and shot into the air and the horse reared up on its hind legs, and he turned and ran off, and as he did he said, 'I am Joaquin.'"

This romantic bandit was said to be the kind of man who couldn't live long without love, and there were many ladies willing to share his company. One in particular was a fiery beauty called Antonia la Molinera. She ran away with him, dressed like a man, and rode with him in the hills. She fought beside him on his raids.

It was said that they were happy for a time. But after awhile she fell in love with another member of Joaquin's gang, and one night she slipped away with him and they disappeared.

Once again Joaquin swore vengeance, and everybody knew he would keep his word. For months he followed their trail from village to village and from ranch to ranch. At last he found the man and killed him. The girl knew her turn would surely come, that she would never be safe until Joaquin was caught; so secretly she sent word to the man who was most likely to capture the bandit, and she told him where Joaquin's hideouts were.

That man was Captain Harry Love, a hunter of men and an adventurer who had come up from Texas. He yearned for the excitement of the hunt and hungered for the reward money that stood on Murieta's head. The state legislature authorized Captain Love to organize a posse of rangers to track down the outlaws and paid them $150 a month, with the rangers furnishing their own horses and outfits.

The orders were to get Joaquin and as many of his gang as possible, and particularly a wanton killer known as Three-Fingered Jack, who was riding with him at the time. Love had learned from the treacherous Antonia where Joaquin's hide-out camps were located, and the long hunt began. The rangers chased the bandits from one camp to another, night and day, through the hills, across the rivers, and over the mountains, gradually closing the circle. Finally, early one morning in July, 1853, the rangers came upon the last camp. Some say they were in the mountains near Tejon Pass in the Tehachapis; or as some researchers claim, the last battle was fought at Cantua Creek in the Diablo Range north of Coalinga. The sun had only half risen, and the crisp dawn was melting into day. The rangers stealthily rode up over a ridge and suddenly, there below them, they saw a little camp hidden in a pocket near a creek in the rugged canyon. One Mexican still lay in his blanket, five were squatting near the fire, where breakfast was being prepared, and some were already eating. A seventh man—bare to the waist, slender, graceful, with dark eyes and long black hair—was standing a little way from the campfire rubbing down a magnificent bay horse. This was Joaquin Murieta.

For a brief moment the scene was frozen in silence. The Mexicans saw the rangers at the same instant they had been seen. No one moved. No one spoke. Joaquin's guns were hanging several feet from where he was standing, just out of reach. Three-Fingered Jack stood back against a rock, watching every move. He was tense and ready. Suddenly Joaquin made a dive for his guns. This was the move that sprung the action. The rangers dug spurs and the posse plunged forward, sweeping down the hill firing as they came. Three-Fingered Jack whipped out his guns and began to fire, but his shots went wild.

The man in the blanket tried to rise, but he was killed immediately. One man by the fire reached for his gun but a bullet struck him in the face and he dropped backward into the burning coals. The others scattered, but one by one they fell. Love and his men charged on Jack, and their lead hit him again and again. He staggered backward from the impact and fell, and was dead.

Joaquin could not reach his guns without moving directly into their fire. In a flash he changed his mind and leaped on his horse. Without saddle or bridle, the horse bounded away over the ridge and up among the rocks. Through the brush and over the hills he flew, with the rangers after him. Joaquin had no gun, only a dagger which he brandished in the air as he pushed the horse on. The rangers were following, shooting as fast as they could. At one precipice, where the rocks hung low overhead, Murieta was scraped off his horse, but he leaped on again and away they went.

Finally, one bullet found flesh, and the horse fell. Joaquin was now on foot. He scrambled through the rocks and behind the bushes. The shots were still coming. Three bullets entered his body, and he staggered. He sank first to his knees, then to his elbows, and finally he lay in the sand. He raised one hand as if to stop the shooting and said, "It is enough. The work is done." And Joaquin Murieta fell dead. The long trail had ended.

This place in the mountains was too far away from town to carry in the dead bodies, but Love had foreseen that situation and had brought along a large sack. Someone in his party cut off the head of Murieta and the hand of Three-Fingered Jack to deliver as proof that they had killed the bandits and thus collect the reward. Later these hideous objects were preserved in jars of alcohol and they were accepted as evidence that the outlaws were dead. On August 18, 1853, the head was placed on exhibition in San Francisco, and the curious were thus enabled to see what was left of the man who but a little while before had been a living legend, Joaquin Murieta, the Robin Hood of El Dorado.

It was the work of only three short years to start the legend. It still lives. The name of Joaquin is seen everywhere in the great valleys of California, and the people say the spirit of Joaquin still rides the California hills. Even a grizzled old poet of the Sierra, Cincinnatus Hiner Miller, in his younger years so admired the hero that he took his name; he became Joaquin Miller and wrote a poem about him. The legend will not die, and wherever unjust laws or greedy men oppress the poor, some Joaquin Murieta or another Robin Hood will ride again.

So much for the legend as the folk remember it. But what became of the bottled head? For years two questions remained unanswered: Was the head in the bottle really that of the bandit Joaquin? And was the specimen really destroyed in 1906, or does it still exist? My quest for the lost head uncovered a story almost as interesting as the legend itself.

As the years passed the story grew. Poets and playwrights put the legend in print. In Fresno an alleged widow of Murieta even surfaced in 1883 to search for the treasure he was supposed to have hidden somewhere. She had spent twenty years looking for it.

Others were searching as well. One American in Mexico got from an old man dying of consumption a map which led him to a place in the Coast Range known as Joaquin's Lookout. Presumably the old man, along with Murieta, Three-Fingered Jack and French Pete had buried the treasure, which consisted of a quicksilver tank full of gold, an oyster can full of watches, and a yeast powder can full of miscellaneous jewelry. After the booty had been securely hidden and the place marked so it could be easily recognized later, Three-Fingered Jack had killed French Pete lest in some drunken spree he would betray the secret hiding place. The American from Mexico, following *el viejo*'s directions, searched but failed to find the cache.

For a while, the location of one of Murieta's hideouts in Mariposa County even became a shrine, and many Mexican and Portuguese families made pilgrimages to it because they believed that sufferers from malarial fever had been miraculously cured there.

Apparently the head in its bottle helped to keep the story alive. In 1906 it was on display in Professor Jordan's Pacific Museum of Anatomy and Science located on Market Street in San Francisco. But it was not lost in the fire as the historians had assumed. A man living near the museum went into the ruins to rummage for what he could find and carried away several items that he considered valuable. Among them was the head. This he stored in his attic where it lay hidden for years. When the old man died and his property was sold, the head was acquired by the Old Town Museum of New Almaden. That the Old Town specimen was the same as the one on exhibit prior to 1906 is attested by a Mr. T. Harris, who wrote a letter to the Old Town Museum saying he had just seen the head there and had recognized it as the one he had seen before the great fire, and he congratulated Old Town on preserving it.

Some time later, a man named Al Keck of Red Bluff obtained it from the Old Town Museum at a bankruptcy sale, and in 1968 it was obtained from Keck by Walter Johnson of Santa Rosa. That it is a genuine human head is of course verifiable. "Soon after I got it," says Johnson, "a man calling himself a doctor came to see it. He took it out and examined it. He said the eyes and hair were real; he even said the blood vessels in the eyes were distended, which would be natural, he said, if the man had died a violent death." Johnson continues, "I wouldn't let him bore into the flesh to sample it. The face is caked with mortician's clay to hold it together, and this doctor said it was the kind of mortician's clay used in the 1880s. Beyond that. I don't know."

According to Jack McAllister of the American Academy McAllister Institute of Funeral Services, New York, a patent was issued in 1868 for a compound composed of plaster of Paris and dehydrated cement to be used as an external pack, but this was much later than the time the head was prepared. Early cosmetics used by women, he reports, did consist of a fine kaolin (clay), and compounds using heavy salts of mercury, arsenic and arsenious acid compounds were not uncommon and would most certainly have been very effective in preserving human tissues. Once thoroughly saturated by these types of compounds, the head could well be preserved through the years.

The question of Murieta the person is still debatable. For the folk the evidence is sufficient, presumably real and believable. For the folklorist the legend provides an interesting case study. For the historian more detective work needs to be done. But however we view it, the story of Joaquin Murieta seems to be California's best and most representative legend.

And for me—I had found the lost head.

II. GHOSTS AND OTHER UNBELIEVABLES

La Llorona

Old tomasito had spent most of his life as a weaver of shawls. Now he lived alone in what was called the Casa Blanca, a Mexican section of Riverside. Everyone knew him and spoke cheerfully to him whenever they saw his frail stooped figure trudging slowly down the street on three legs, for the walking stick which he had made himself was almost as big as his own thin limbs. On this night in February he was making his way to the home of an old friend, Lupe Flores, where he knew he would enjoy warm food, a good drink, and the pleasant conversation of friends. Every Sunday night in winter, guests of all ages would drop in and partake of the hospitality of Mrs. Flores and perhaps sing a little and talk about Mexico, or repeat the latest jokes of Father Rios, or speculate on the reckless escapades of the younger generation.

As usual he found several people there. He knew most of them, but some he did not recognize. It was getting that way now. He didn't know as many people as he used to, and the talk was not always to his liking. That's how it seemed this night; the refreshments were good and the house was warm, but the talk was cold and dark.

The words were about death. The newspaper that day had carried the story of a terrible automobile accident, perhaps the worst in the history of Riverside. Five young men, all known to the guests assembled, had been killed on Victoria Avenue. Their car, going seventy-five miles an hour, had struck a palm tree and the wreck was total. The tragedy had spread a cloud of sadness over the entire Mexican section. Grief and shock, but not surprise.

"I knew it was sure to happen," Mrs. Flores was saying. "It had to happen, if not today then tomorrow. There was no way to make the curse go away." Everyone agreed, and a cold chill tightened the back of Tomasito's neck. He, too, knew that the fate of the boys had been inevitable, for they had looked upon the face and seen the baleful eyes of the dreaded Llorona. Something evil had to follow.

"It was only night before last that two of them saw her," someone in the group was saying. The boys had reported that at about midnight on Victoria south of Maude Street they had seen a lone woman walking on the dark sidewalk wearing a long white dress that shimmered in the shadows. They had hurried toward her, thinking to tease her a little, but when she turned to face them she was crying. She stared at them like one with *mal ojo*, the evil eye, and then she vanished. They knew they had seen La Llorona, the weeping woman.

"It's hard to believe in anything like La Llorona these days," someone said. "Did anybody here ever see her?" Old Tomasito squirmed a little and pushed back further into his corner. He had never seen her himself, but all his life he had heard about her. She was like the bogey man that parents used to frighten children. "If you don't behave, La Llorona will come and get you," they would say. And he knew that in every place where she was seen, something terrible would happen. His memory raced from one story to another, old in the telling, and now if she was here in this neighborhood—well, he would rather not hear about it on a night like this when he had to walk home alone.

"I never saw her myself," Mrs. Flores was saying, "but I know people who have. She comes from way back in history, many years ago, when the Spaniards were in Mexico, in the days of cape and sword. As the story goes, there was a beautiful young girl but she was very poor, and her house was where only the peons lived. She fell in love with a rich and powerful Spanish don, and she had three children that were his. She wanted him to marry her, but he wouldn't because she was beneath him. He married someone else. But he wanted to string her along, and he said that if she didn't have the children to disgrace him, well, maybe." Mrs. Flores held her audience with the old story.

"So she killed the three little ones to prove her love for him. One by one she drowned them in the river. When he married another, she went mad with grief. She would wander the streets alone at night, looking for her children and wailing over their death. People were afraid to see her coming. And the man then decided that he loved her and was sorry, but it was too late. She had put a curse on him, and in a duel his sword failed him and he died. But she could not die. Or maybe she did die, but her ghost would not find rest. She went on through the years, weeping and wailing, and looking for her dead children, and she goes on to this day. They say that when she appears, someone will die."

Old Tomasito felt a chill and pulled his coat tightly around him. He knew this sad story well, and he had heard the song that people often sang to express the feelings of a distraught lover who had seen her. It was a beautiful song, but mournful. The thought of it made him uncomfortable, for in his youth he had learned it himself, and as if the devil had put the thought there he had even, at times, secretly wished that he might see and perhaps comfort this beautiful, tortured, unearthly creature.

The group must have caught his secret thought, for someone picked up a guitar and began to sing the haunting old ballad. He listened, but his mind could not hold parts of the song and the words slipped through and were lost, but a few verses and the refrain echoed in his mind.

> You were leaving the church one day, Llorona,
>   when I passed and saw you.
> You were wearing a beautiful *huipil,*
>   and I believed that you were the Virgin.
>
> Alas for me, Llorona, Llorona, Llorona of a white lily,
> Those who don't know about love, Llorona
>   don't know what martyrdom is.
>
> They say I have no grief, Llorona, because
>   they don't see me weeping.
> The dead make no noise at all, Llorona,
>   and they have a greater pain.
>
> Alas for me, Llorona, Llorona of long ago and today.
> Long ago I was something marvelous to see;
>   today I am not even a shadow.
>
>   Pain and what is not pain, alas, Llorona,
>   All is pain for me.
>   Yesterday I wept to see you, alas Llorona,
>   And today I weep because I saw you.

The refrain ended and the people sat for a moment in silence. Then the party broke up, and the guests gradually departed to find their way home, taking their heavy thoughts with them. As the last guest was leaving he noticed that the old man still sat half hidden in the shadows. "You should go home now, *viejo,*" he said softly. "Don't be afraid. La Llorona will not be looking for you tonight—unless you have done something that would remind her of her false lover."

The old man's mind flashed back to his days of strength and pride, and he trembled a little. Without a word he rose, made a slight bow of thanks to his friend Mrs. Flores, and tapped his heavy cane out into the darkness. What his thoughts were as he slowly made his way down the deserted street, no one would know.

It was near midnight when he reached Grace Street. The moon was rising, and the cold clear winter night seemed to come alive with moving shadows. He was near the place where fire had destroyed a home, and he could see the dead, sightless windows and the skeleton chimney of the ruined house that stood like a ghostly remnant from centuries ago rising out of its own grave. He tried to walk a little faster, but the stick grew heavy in his hands.

In the misty yard something was moving. It glided out of the shadows and was coming toward him. In the faint moonlight he could see that it was the figure of a woman. He wanted to run, but his legs would not move. Like a small animal held in the spell of a snake's glittering eye, he stopped still and tried to listen. The moving figure stopped with him, and a faint sound seemed to come from it. When he found the strength again he started to walk as fast as his thin legs and cane could carry him. The specter also began to move again, not as if to overtake him but to keep the same distance between them. It was a woman with a tall, graceful figure. Her long dress was a shining white, faintly glistening in the silver moonlight. He could see her long black hair hanging halfway down her back, and when she moved it was with the graceful gliding step of a dancer. In an earlier time he would have thought, "What a beautiful woman she is," but tonight was different. Her head was bowed as if she was looking always at the ground, but he knew she had seen him. He could hear the heavy beating of his own heart. Then again came that other sound from somewhere outside himself. It was a long low moan of agony.

The old man was cold and trembling, but he couldn't run. Again he stopped, as if pulled back by a relentless unseen force. He lifted his heavy stick and raised his other hand, palm outward, as if to ward off an attack. The ghostly figure stopped and raised its head toward him. The face was wrenched with pain, and the eyes glowed red like coals of fire. Suddenly the wailing stopped, and with a piercing shriek the woman moved toward him. A sharp pain tore through his chest. He felt dizzy. The cane slipped from his hand, and he crumbled to the ground.

No one knows how long he lay there, but when he was found he was rushed to the hospital. "They took him to the emergency," Mrs. Flores reported later. "He was conscious, and he told them what had happened. And then he died. They said it was his bad heart. Maybe it was. . . . Maybe."

The Ghost Ship of the Desert

IF I TOLD YOU about a ghost ship marooned in the sands of the desert east of the old Salton Sea, and that it might contain a fortune in pearls, would you believe it? A lot of people did about a hundred years ago, and it is said that at one time the Indians had a legend about it. The ghostly skeleton of a lost ship sailing the desert sand hundreds of miles from the ocean? It has been reported many times, and expeditions have been formed to search for it, but it has never quite been reached. As elusive and spectral as any other ghost, it has been described, and its eerie presence has excited the imaginations of many old prospectors and desert rats; yet whether it is real or only a phantom like the legendary *Flying Dutchman*, or an apparition shaped by the heat and light of the desert, or merely a romantic fantasy no one knows. Or perhaps it could be real.

Old rumors still echo through the lonely desert carrying tales of how the mystery ship got there and of a vast treasure stowed away in its decaying hulk. One report is that in the year 1610 the King of Spain sent a small naval expedition to hunt for pearls off the western coast of Mexico. Three ships went out from Acapulco. The divers were successful, and their brass-studded chests gradually filled with pearls. When no more could be found, the Spaniards continued to accumulate the priceless treasure by trading with the Indians.

Of the three ships that went out, one returned to Acapulco, one was caught in a terrible storm and sank taking its fortune with it, and the third sailed up into the Gulf of California. At the northern end of the Gulf there was a narrow passage with currents indicating that a river was flowing southward, and up the river after a great distance the shores widened to form a vast inland sea. Here the little ship was trapped. It sailed around in this shallow ocean for some time, but eventually the water receded and the desperate vessel could not get out. Finally the ship was grounded. The doomed crew perished, either from natural causes or at the hands of the Indians, and the desolate ship with its useless sails hanging limp and its glistening treasure still hidden below remained a solitary corpse to rot in the mud and encroaching sand of the old Salton Sea.

The Indians of the region, on winter nights when the old ones remembered strange things from bygone days, used to tell a story about a great ship that came in with the floods over the desert and remained like a bird in the sand, and after awhile its white wings drooped and blew away leaving only its skeleton with some bones standing up like tall tree stumps. After the passing of time, the old Indians said, the sand blew in and covered the parching form, but someday the dunes would move on and leave the skeleton standing bare as it did before.

Both the origin of the ghost ship and its exact location have never been fully established. Old prospectors, explorers, and writers never could come up with quite the same story, and the mystery drifted into legend. One reporter for a San Bernardino newspaper allegedly investigated the rumors based on the experience of a man named Charley Clusker, who had taken a party out into the desert to locate the ship. One member of the expedition gave his explanation: "In the year 1862 some of us had mining interests in La Paz, Arizona. We had a skiff built in Los Angeles. She was twenty-one feet long, rigged with a single mast for sailing, and mounted on wheels for the overland haul to the Colorado River. All went well until we had crossed the San Gorgonio pass and come to the lowest point in the desert. There the teams gave out and we were forced to abandon her. That was the origin of the ship of the desert." But other investigators said no.

In 1870 the story of the phantom ship was still being reported. A man named Albert Evans said he had seen it, and his account was quoted by the newspapers. Like the Ancient Mariner he was eager to tell his tale: "By two o'clock I had reached the summit of the divide between Dos Palmas and the Palma Seca, and looked into the plain. Southward to the very horizon stretched a great plain of snowy salt, the white ghost of a dead sea which once covered all this accursed land but has passed away forever. Across this white plain, as across the waters of a placid lake, the moon threw a track of shimmering light. Right in this burning pathway of light, far out in the center of the ghostly sea, lay what appeared in the distance to be the wreck of a gallant ship, which might have gone down three centuries ago."

Such a tale was sure to arouse the imagination of anyone with a thirst for adventure and possibly treasure. The excitement spread and a party was soon organized to cross the desert in search of the lost ship. When they came back they said they had found it. They had no pearls to show, but they did divulge its location, which was forty miles north of the San Bernardino and Fort Yuma road, and thirty miles west of Dos Palmas. There they had found the wreck of a large vessel imbedded in the sand, they said. Nearly one-third of the forward part was plainly visible. The stump of the bowsprit remained, and portions of the timbers were well preserved.

Other expeditions set forth to verify these reports, but they came back disappointed. The phantom ship had moved, or the shifting salt and sand had buried it once again. The newspapers took a cautious position on the story, as if they hoped it was true but didn't dare say so. One editor wrote, "We do not propose to adapt any theory in regard to it; it may or may not date back to the time of Cortez, but it certainly furnishes abundant matter for speculation."

It was now time for the scientists to tackle the question. A conference was held in which the mystery was examined. One professor named Hanks read a carefully prepared report on the subject in which he summarized all the published accounts of the sightings and then added the versions he had obtained from interviews and correspondence. He produced positive testimony that many persons had seen, at a distance of a few miles, an object that they believed to be the wreck of a large ship embedded in the sand. All this was only hearsay, but it was enough to disturb the scientific mind of Mr. Hanks. He concluded his report with a theoretical explanation that the alleged ship may be only a mass of the curious travertine which forms the alkaline lakes on the plains and southern deserts, and which grows into fantastic shapes like coral.

Another professor went into the matter of the geography of the region, parts of which are below sea level and other parts as much as seven hundred fifty feet in elevation. He concluded that the presumed location of the ship was about seventy feet lower than the ocean. The story of the Spanish treasure ship, therefore, was topographically possible.

And finally, Colonel Evans was asked to repeat the account of his own experience previously reported. He had crossed the desert several times, had seen the object once from a distance of ten miles and afterwards from about three miles, and he had examined it with a glass. It appeared to be the hulk of a vessel, partly on its side and partly buried in the alkaline mud that surrounded it. The locality was a salt plain which at certain seasons was covered with water and at others quite dry. He had heard the Indian story of the ship, and he repeated the native legend that the ocean once flowed in here from the Gulf. He could not swear that what he had seen was a ship, but he thought it was.

The scientific world had been agitated by the legend, and other expeditions went forth like searchers for the lost Ark of Noah. The years passed, and the mud and salt of the lowlands dried into a flaky gray crust that glistened in the sunlight, and the sands of the desert highlands drifted into dunes that slowly crawled and shifted, humping to the will of the hot desert wind. But the story was not forgotten. In 1878 the elusive ship was reported again. It seems that late one summer two German prospectors, barely alive, staggered into Yuma from the Colorado desert. From thirst, hunger, and exhaustion their miserable bodies had withered into ghostly spectres like creatures from another world. Their story, when they could tell it, was as strange as their appearance.

The prospectors had gone out in search for minerals in the rocky slopes skirting the south and west sides of the San Bernardino range. Three had started, but only two survived. At a point about a hundred miles northwest of Yuma one of the three had ventured from camp alone to search for something they had seen the night before. He never returned.

What they had seen was a weird apparition. The time was just about sundown, and they were camped among the rocks on the hardpan of the desert floor. They all saw it—an immense ship under full sail, which seemed to float before them as a cloud until it disappeared into the sunset. With awe and wonder they had talked about it that night, and the next day their companion set out to investigate it. When he failed to come back, they concluded that he found the vessel and then by some supernatural power he had been taken aboard and shanghaied to another world where time and space knew no laws of nature.

The story of the two prospectors was too wild for the good people of Yuma to believe. They laughed and called the old men fools. And yet—could it be true? Even the most preposterous occurrences should be investigated. So the next day two men and three Indian guides set out to search for the missing man. After several days in the desert they found what remained of the lost prospector. He had died of thirst. His corpse lay prone under the scorching rays of the sun, and for some inexplicable reason it was naked. But no sign of the phantom ship was seen.

Several years later a writer for the San Francisco *Examiner* joined an expedition for the purpose of finding the answer, once and for all, to the mystery of the legend. Under the leadership of a certain Tom Brown of Arizona, the group included a Nick Walford and others identified only as Jack and Charley. On February 14, 1882, the expedition left Yuma fully equipped for a three-week trip. To convey the excitement of the adventure, the reporter told his story in the first person:

"A more favorable season could not have been selected for making the journey. As the trip was being made only for pleasure and out of sheer curiosity, it was on the sixteenth day before the party reached a point about one hundred twenty miles northwest of Yuma and about forty miles directly east of Indio.

"Provisions were running short, owing to failure to encounter any game, and the water burros were loaded for a three days' trip, with the intention of making for the railroad which, it was calculated, could be reached in that time. A dry camp was made on the desert some ten miles from the mountains and fully thirteen miles from the spring at which we had taken water. An early supper was had, and shortly before sunset Nick Walford and Jack set out to drive the burros to a patch of grass which had been crossed half a mile back of the spot where camp had been pitched. The short twilight of that region had just begun, and I was busy in making down the beds when startled by an exclamation of Tom Brown.

"'By George!' he yelled. 'There she is. Look!' Turning around and casting my eyes in the direction which his hand indicated I saw the outlines of a sailing vessel. Every portion of her was clearly defined, yet a haze or a peculiar indescribable light was cast upon the scene. It was too late an hour for a mirage; besides this, the view was not stationary. The craft was moving rapidly on its course with all sails set. Apparently she was about half a mile distant and stood quarter to us. The vessel, I judged, was about eighty feet in length, eighteen feet breadth of beam, and of about forty tons burden. The hull sat well out of the water—which was plainly visible—while the bow rose straight above the deck. The stern also sat high out of the water after the fashion of Chinese junks, and the two masts, fore and aft rigged, gave the strange vessel a very odd appearance, unlike anything I had ever yet seen. The decks projected beyond the hull after the manner of those of the old Roman galleys, but undoubtedly the vessel was of more modern construction and probably belonged to the sixteenth century.

"As strange and startling as was the weird scene, I was more than astonished at the sounds I heard. The creaking, straining noise of a sailing vessel running before a stiff breeze was plainly heard, while the distant notes of a sailor's song fell upon my ear.

"The discharge of a rifle near at hand, followed by a lusty halloa, distracted our attention from the vision, and we hastily answered the signal. A few moments afterward, Walford and Jack walked into camp, explaining that they had lost their directions in returning, and fired the shot to attract our attention. Brown and I turned from our companions to again view the mysterious ship, but it had disappeared as suddenly as it had appeared. Darkness was upon us."

Today, after more than a hundred years, the legend is remembered by a few rock hounds and other adventurous campers who still like to explore this desert waste. Countless aircrafts of all kinds have flown over the area without reporting anything more fantastic than the naturally grotesque forms left on the landscape by the natural processes of erosion. You could say there was never a ship there at all, and that what those ancient witnesses saw was only an illusion. Or, if you believe in legends, you might say that the old ship really came, and died, and left its ghost to haunt the desolate wasteland, doomed to continue its endless search for a way out until it can eventually get back to the sea where old ships settle into their proper watery graves and their souls can find rest. And perhaps the skeleton hulk is only buried for the present, only to reappear when time and the shifting of the desert sand will strip it bare and reveal it once again with the gleaming light of sunset streaking through its bare ribs, and its chest of pearls still hidden in its bosom.

Bloodstain

MOST PEOPLE, at least once in their lives, have experienced some kind of supernatural phenomenon. Sometimes it confronts us unexpectedly and with such surrealistic distortion that the effect is sheer terror. So it is for young Tom Moungovin as he lies in the dark of night on an old iron bed in a crypt-like room of a long-abandoned, half-decayed mansion. His eyes are on the door, which is latched tight, but he knows that in a moment that door will squeak open and something will enter the room, and no human power or earthly force can prevent it from happening.

The story began back in the mid-1880s when an Englishman named Phelps came to California and bought a large cattle ranch some twenty miles in from the Mendocino Coast. He had money, and to express his taste for elegance he built a beautiful mansion. With all its Victorian gingerbread trimmings and the well-planned gardens surrounding it, it stood as a reminder to him of a good life past and a symbol of status in the rough new world despite the fact that it was grotesquely out of time and place in this lonely, rugged, mountainous back-country of the American far west.

His modish and expensive furniture was shipped around Cape

Horn and freighted in by wagon from the coast. A piano, books, carpets, and numerous what-nots for the assorted bric-a-brac were not overlooked. When the mansion was finished and everything was in place, Phelps decided to give a big house-warming party. For the evening feast, half a steer was wrapped in gunny sacks and buried in a pit and surrounded by hot coals to be covered with dirt, there to roast for five or six hours. Wide boards were laid across saw horses in the back yard to serve as picnic tables, and a generous variety of liquid refreshments were made ready on the porch.

Everyone within messenger range was invited. Miners from the mountains, loggers, ranchers, fishermen from the coast, and even the schoolteachers were notified, and all were eager to come and see this latest wonder of the new world and partake of the Phelps hospitality. They arrived, bringing their families in wagons, buggies, and on horseback to assemble for an evening of high society and convivial homage to their new neighbor.

All came, that is, except one man. That morning old man McInturf had had a quarrel with his son-in-law, and the latter in a fit of anger refused to accompany the old man to the party, but instead he had muttered some vague threats of "getting even" and disappeared into the woods to brood over his grievances, whatever they might have been. But as the tough Old Mac had been heard to say on several occasions, "Anybody ever tries to kill me, I'll take him with me. Or come back and get him."

Late that afternoon the beef was dug out of the hot pit and served in thick juicy slices along with the other gastronomic marvels that made it a veritable banquet, which was duly washed down and enhanced by virtue of the ample supply of potable reinforcements. Later in the evening everybody went into the large front room, the carpets were rolled back, the fiddlers tuned up, and a Virginia reel was started.

Near the hour of midnight the dancing stopped. The fiddlers had declared a recess for refueling, and the people were strolling or talking in little groups in the flower garden or gossiping on the porch. Then all at once, for some inexplicable reason, the group fell silent. This in itself is not an unusual phenomenon. There are times at any party when all the talk and noise reach a pause, and everyone for a moment is suspended in silence. The old folk used to say that's when an angel has entered the room. But this silence was different, ominous, not comfortable for angels or mortals.

Out of the stillness came the sound of hoofbeats. A rider was racing up the lane toward the house. Some people later remembered that it was a big white horse, and the rider wore a long black cloak that floated out in the wind behind him. Others said the horse was black, and he came so fast his feet scarcely touched the ground. The rider drew rein at the edge of the circle of light from the lanterns on the porch, and old man McInturf, thinking it was his son-in-law who had finally decided to come to the party, stepped down off the porch toward him and called out, "Hey, George! Is that you?"

For answer came the blast of a gun. The old man, shot in the throat and chest, staggered and fell. Before anyone could see who it was, the rider whirled around and disappeared in the darkness down the lane. McInturf was bleeding badly, and his friends dragged him up on the porch. An irregular pool of blood formed under his head. With a hideous coughing, gurgling sound in his throat, the old man died.

They took the body in and laid it on a canvas spread over the sofa. Then some of the Phelps's hired help got a bucket, and with soap and water they washed the blood from the floorboards of the porch. The party ended, and in respectful silence the people went their separate ways.

The next morning a wagon was backed up to the front of the house, and the body of the old man was carried out of the living room, across the porch, and loaded into the makeshift hearse. But as the body passed over the place where the old man died, a ruddy brown stain began to form, fresh and damp, exactly as it had been the night before.

Again they applied soap and water, and the ugly pattern was

erased. But that was not to be the end of it. Several weeks later, so it was said, the same figure began to reappear. No matter how scrupulously the boards were cleansed, after a time that irregular dark brown design would gradually emerge again. A fresh coat of paint was put on, and for a while it was thought the curse had been lifted. But eventually, through the paint, the same brown pattern began to show.

It was said that McInturf's son-in-law, in the county jail awaiting trail, died of a blood clot in the brain. Not long after that, a young man working for the Phelps family was sent to the insane asylum, and it was rumored that his madness came on suddenly, all in one night, the night he claimed he saw something so terrible that his head almost exploded. Word quickly got around that the place was haunted.

For various "normal" reasons Mr. Phelps sold the ranch and moved away. Years passed, and the place went from one owner to another until it eventually became the property of one of the big lumber companies at Fort Bragg. The mansion had been abandoned long since, and after many years of neglect it had taken on the appearance of death and decay. People were convinced, now, that a curse was on it. Strange sounds and moving lights were reported in the house, and people said that old McInturf's ghost was still looking for revenge.

Occasionally a party of deer hunters would try to use the spectral old mansion as a camp, but it was said that no one ever stayed there beyond midnight. However fortified the deer hunters might be with guns and liquid courage, at some time during the night they always developed urgent business elsewhere and departed without delay.

More years went by, and the old house in the hills was almost forgotten. But one young man had heard the stories and could not put them out of his mind. Tom lived in Fort Bragg, but his job with the lumber company was to look after the various properties of the company to see that the fences were up, gates were closed, water holes were open for the cattle on the ranches, and in general to be caretaker for thousands of acres of ranch and timber land. This frequently took him into the foothills. He made his circuits on horseback with only a dog for company, often camping wherever he might be when night came.

Late one afternoon he was in the vicinity of the old Phelps property, and remembering the stories about the haunted house he began to wonder what would happen if he spent the night there. In fact, he had made the brag to several of his friends that he would spend a night there, sooner or later, come hell or high water. If the stories were true, and if he should actually see the ghost, well, he too might go mad. But of course that was all just nonsense. Or was it? He didn't believe in ghosts, anyway. Or did he? Certainly there was something that seemed to be drawing him toward the answer to his question. So it was more in apprehension than mere curiosity that he at last turned his horse into the old Phelps Lane in the foothills.

It was dusk when he reached the yard and saw the old house. A sad relic of the past, he thought, like so many rusty, useless, "throwed-away" things from pioneer times. The picket fence was sagging, the front gate was clinging by one hinge, weeds and wild grass filled the space where roses once had bloomed, and the apple trees had long since dried away to death and turned to skeletons. The house itself was only a distorted reflection of its former self. The porch sagged, several window panes were broken, and the paint was peeling off leaving splotches of bare wood that had faded and softened to gray velvet in the hot sun of summer and its freezing storms of winter.

Tom watered his horse at the old well, tied him to a fir tree out back, and fed him some grain that he carried in one of the saddle-bags. He untied his blanket from behind the saddle, pulled his rifle from its scabbard, took a small sack of food from the other saddle-bag, and built a small campfire on a bare spot in the front yard. Then with his rolled-up blanket over one shoulder he crossed the porch and entered the house. A few scraps of broken furniture remained in the large front room. From there a narrow hallway led to some bedrooms that were bare, dirty, and coldly indifferent to human presence.

One bedroom still retained its privacy by token of a fairly substantial door that opened and shut with squeaking resistance. Inside, Tom found one useful piece of furniture. It was an iron bedstead, the kind that used to be so stylish, with curiously carved head and foot pieces. The springs were rusty but substantial, and on these he rolled out his blanket. Here he would spend the night, if not comfortably, at least without any chance of human intrusion. He was used to the solitary life, and the prospect of being the only human occupant of the lonely house and in a sense possessing it for a few hours morbidly appealed to him.

Out in the yard again, he made some coffee, leisurely ate his meal, fed the dog, and rolled a smoke. It was dark now, and the night sounds began to float in around him. His dog, a large hairy creature of unspecified origin but with a reputation for vicious hostility to any man or beast other than his master, quietly settled down beside him. So far, there was apparently nothing to fear, and yet he couldn't shake the uneasy feeling that he was not alone.

When drowsiness came, Tom picked up his rifle and entered the house. He thought he must be some kind of fool to be there, and yet he was there. The darkness tightened around him. Well, he thought, this is it. There can be no backing out now.

The dog followed him into the bedroom. He closed the door, though he scarcely knew why, except that bedroom doors ought to be closed. And just for the hell of it he latched it with the wooden bar he found attached to the door at one end so it could drop down and fit into a bracket nailed to the solid jamb. It was dark outside, so the one window of the room was of little use, but the shadowy outline of the bed was there. He leaned his gun against the wall and stretched out on his blanket. The dog curled up on the floor beside the bed, and before long Tom was asleep.

He couldn't remember how long he had slept, perhaps two hours or more, when he was awakened by the dog. Whining and snarling, the animal was standing erect and trembling. In the faint shadows Tom could see that the dog was frightened by something beyond the bedroom door. Tom stiffened and listened. Faintly out of the silence he heard, from somewhere in the hall outside, a muffled thump...thump...thump..., like a slow, cautious footstep. The sound stopped by the door. Then came another kind of sound—a hoarse, gurgling, choking cough. The dog, with a low growl, retreated toward the window.

"Cheough...cheough!" came the sound in the hall. And then, very slowly, the door began to open. Tom waited, tense. The coughing had ceased. Nothing. A slight waft of cool air blew gently across the room, but nothing more. The dog slowly relaxed, and Tom sensed that whatever it was had gone away. He realized, then, that his heart was still pounding and he was trembling.

He got up and in the half darkness he groped his way out into the hallway. All was quiet. He went through the living room and looked out into the yard. Nothing alive was there except his horse, who gave him a low whinney of welcome recognition. Tom half thought he had been dreaming, that it had been only a nightmare. Was the thing reaching for his sanity, too, like the others? He knew he should get out of there, and yet he was committed to see it through; he had to go back.

Again in the bedroom he closed and bolted the door. He then carefully tied a piece of twine around the latch, fastening the door securely from the inside. This done, he found his bed again and lay down. The dog settled back on the floor, and everything was as it had been before.

For a long time Tom was too tense to sleep. He listened for the slightest sound, but there was none. Gradually his mind drifted off into a restless dream, and two more hours went by. It was near midnight when he awoke again, startled once more by the dog. He noticed that the moon had come up. Shining dimly through the window, its dark yellow light cast weird shadows on the flowery wallpaper that hung torn from the wall in grotesque patches.

The dog was quivering. His eyes again were staring at the door. The hair stood up on the back of his neck, his teeth were bared, and a gutteral snarl came from his throat. Tom sat up against the bedstead, cold and tense. His head was throbbing as if it would explode. He could feel the pulse in his temples and hear it in his ears.

Thump...thump...thump came the sound again in the hall. It stopped just outside the door. Then he heard the choking cough, "Cheough...cheough!" The door slowly began to squeak open.

With an almost human cry, the dog *crashed* through the window and ran for the hills. Tom followed the dog. He spent the rest of the night beside his horse under the fir tree.

The next morning he came back into the deserted house. The bedroom door was open, and he went in and retrieved his gun and blanket. As he came back out of the front room, crossing the porch, he noticed something he had not seen the night before. There on the boards was a fresh dark brown stain forming an irregular pattern.

The Lady of the Lake

It WAS THE LAST wagon train to make its way into California that year. Because of accidents and miscalculations their crossing had been delayed and they had fallen far behind in their schedule. In midsummer they had made it over the Rockies at South Pass; by late summer they had followed the Humboldt River as far as Winnemucca, where the trail divided. Instead of turning south to the Truckee, they chose to avoid the perilous Sierra crossing, which had proved fatal to the Donner party in 1846, and instead they took the old Applegate Trail which led northwest across the Nevada desert. Their plan was to cross the Warner mountains into the northeastern tip of California and proceed to Goose Lake. There the immigrant trail split again, the north fork heading on to Oregon and the south fork swinging around on the old Lassen trail to enter the upper Sacramento Valley. It was the latter route they had chosen.

No one remembers their names. How many wagons were in the train or how many families with young children they had among them would be meaningless statistics now, long since forgotten. It is known that one member of the party was a girl of about sixteen, but whether she was beautiful or plain no one can tell—or whether she was happy or melancholy of disposition, light or dark of complexion, or if she was in love with a young man in the next wagon.

The causes of their delay do not matter. The significant fact is that it was autumn before they were able to drag their way across the rugged mountains and twist down the west side into California. On their second day in the Promised Land they reached the level country that spreads to Goose Lake in Modoc County. The fatigue of the mountain's defiance was still heavy on them, and this last day's distance had been long because they were in a deadly race against the approaching storms of winter.

They camped for the night by a small lake—or little more than a slough, actually. They drew their wagons into a circle as usual, more from habit than from any serious concern about a possible Indian attack. All the way across Nevada they had taken this precaution, for although Chief Winnemucca and his Paiutes had been peaceful enough, there were always renegade bands to be feared. Each night a guard had been posted to warn the travelers of any approaching danger, but now they were in California where Indian raids on wagon trains were not to be expected, so on this night no guard was posted.

Weary from the day's travel they built their campfires. A cold wind was blowing in from the north, and dark clouds were forming. The winter storms would come early that year, and remembering the story of the Donner party that had perished in the early snows of the Sierra they were thankful to be near the end of their journey. With fingers stiffened by the cold they took care of their animals, prepared their evening meal, and ate in silence. The young girl did her part, as usual, preparing the meal, cleaning and stacking the utensils for use in the morning, and spreading the quilts in the wagon for the night's bed.

As darkness closed in, the rain came. The people crawled into their covered wagons for the night and tied the flaps securely against the chilling wind. By midnight the sleet had turned to snow, and in the darkness a ghostly white was spreading over the sagebrush and outcroppings of lava rock around them.

Slowly dawn came, dull and gray. The snow was now four or five inches deep, and its thickening blanket had obliterated the trail completely and all else but the boldest of landmarks. In that moment of half-light before the cold dawn, the covered wagons seemed to huddle closer in their little circle like shivering creatures lost on a faraway whitening plain. The people had not yet stirred. It was as if for a moment the little camp was a picture frozen in time. This was the moment that the Indians chose for attack.

They rode over the hills from the east, paused for an instant to survey the scene, and then put heels to their horses. Whooping and yelling they rode in, brandishing their rifles. As the startled immigrants tumbled out of their wagons in confusion they were shot down. Men, women, and children fell as the Indian rifles cracked, and their blood etched red splotches in the snow.

The young girl jumped out of her wagon and began to run. She was wearing a white flannel nightgown, and in the tumult she got away. The white gown camouflage shielded her, and unnoticed she ran in her bare feet through the snow. She circled the small lake and crouched behind a large sagebrush on the other side. There she could hear the shrieks of her family and friends as they fell, and could see the attackers with axes and clubs finish off their victims. She watched the flames as the wagons and all their contents were burned. The horses and cattle were driven off, the food was either destroyed or carried away, and the clothing that had not been burned was put on and worn in mock grandeur by the frenzied pillagers.

With the full light of dawn, the work was finished and the attackers with whoops and antics of bravado left the scene of devastation and death. The girl, now so cold she could scarcely move her limbs, came back. Nothing remained alive. The food was gone; the animals had been taken away. She was alone in this endless white wilderness. All signs of the wagon trail had been obliterated by the snow, but that mattered little; she would not have known which way to go even if she could have undertaken the journey. The fatal camp was miles from any settlement. No one would come along this trail to find her, for theirs had been the last wagon train of the year; it would be months before anyone would venture this way again, and winter had closed in.

No one knows how many days she stayed at that desolate camp searching for scraps of clothing to wrap around her and poking for bits of food that might remain in the debris. In an old half-burnt Bible she scribbled a few brief words of her story. Then, from exposure and starvation, she died and the heavy winter snows piled in and buried the whole scene.

When spring finally came and the snow melted, some ranchers found the remains of the camp and pieced together the story. But the people whose bones lay there meant nothing to them, and soon the ghastly discovery was no longer news in the far-flung settlements of the region. Years passed, and the incident gradually faded from memory—except for one weird circumstance that would not go away.

Northeastern California was ideal range land. The grass grew thick and tall in that high lava-streaked plateau country, and both sheep and cattle could be accommodated there. Ditches were dug and sinks were scraped out to be made into reservoirs for watering the range stock during the drought of summer. So it naturally happened that the little lake beside which the wagon train had ended its tragic journey became a reservoir.

Two or three generations came and went, and the sheep and cattle prospered. But through the years, that one spot had had a bad name. At first, no one paid much attention to the stories, but eventually word got around that a ghost lived in that lake. Cowboys reported that the cattle found the water distasteful. Basque sheepherders told of strange lights that flickered around the place at night, and at certain times of the year they could hear the long wailing cry of a woman echoing out of the darkness across the water. They began to avoid the place, and the grass, ungrazed, grew more lush than ever.

Eventually it was decided that these rumors had to be stopped. Perhaps if someone spent the night there and reported that these phenomena, if they existed at all, had a natural explanation, then all that ghost nonsense would be laid to rest. So a young man was found for the experiment. He was one of those go-anywhere-do-anything types of cowboy who represented the last of their species on the western range. Give him a horse, a gun, a rope, a tightly rolled blanket, and a saddlebag packed with grub, and he and his kind were able to function as independent and totally self-sufficient organisms schooled in the ways of nature, dedicated to personal freedom, and inspired by a taste for adventure. Our cowboy, thus equipped and motivated, took the job and, like a medieval knight in armor, set forth on his quest.

It was just about sunset when he reached the reservoir. He tied his horse to a sagebrush, spread out his blanket, built a fire, ate his supper, and settled down for the night. With his saddle for a pillow and his gun within easy reach he stretched out on the blanket at the water's edge and rolled a cigarette. Coyotes began to howl in the distance, and he took pleasure in the wild melancholy music of the night. The long wail of a lonely hunter drifted in, to be answered in a few moments by the rapid series of echoing notes of a coyote bitch from somewhere in the rocks nearby. Then came, over and over again, the sharp high tremolo of yapping howls of the young pups from their den somewhere in the low cliffs a half mile away. These were familiar sounds, and the cowboy relaxed to the rude comfort of the place. All that rigamarole about ghosts on this lake was probably just nonsense made up by those lazy Basque sheepherders.

The cowboy was stretched out on the very spot where once lay the frozen bodies of the massacre victims.

Night deepened and the cowboy dozed off. For a few hours he slept soundly, but toward midnight he returned to half consciousness, twisting and turning on his blanket. Suddenly he sat up, startled into full wakefulness by a noise that was different from the normal sounds of the range. This was no coyote howling in the distance; it came from across the lake, and was more like a human cry.

He listened. The long wail, sad and low, drifted unmistakably from across the lake. In the half darkness he could discern what looked like a clump of brush on the other side. He hadn't noticed it before, but there it was, a large sagebrush, and it was from there that the chilling sound came.

Then there was something else. A tiny spot of light seemed to grow out of the bush. Instead of shifting to right or left, it wavered up and down slightly and then began to glide directly across the water toward him.

He waited and watched. His horse, tied to a bush behind him, snorted and began to pull back on his rope. Whatever it was, the animal had seen it too, and wanted to get away.

The light moved slowly up and down, back and forth, and always toward him a few feet above the water. It grew gradually larger as it came. About midway across the lake the yellowish-red sphere of light paused, suspended. It was large enough now to reveal something else. Inside the ball of light the figure of a woman was beginning to take form. Again the melancholy wail floated in. The horse tugged at his rope, and the cowboy fumbled for his gun. His hand shook as he pulled the trigger. Several times he fired directly into the bubble of light, but nothing changed. The figure remained and grew bigger and bigger as its flaming circle came closer.

It was a woman with long straggly hair, wrapped in a whitish gown, and her arms were moving. As the light and the woman it carried neared the shore of the lake, she stretched forth her arms like a child reaching for help. The horse tore loose from his tether and bolted away. The cowboy followed the horse.

He did not return for his saddle or blanket or gun. The next

"She stretched forth her arms like a child reaching for help."

morning the bareback rider came into town and reported what he had seen. He was paid off and left town, and his story was hushed up. Eventually the reservoir returned to normal, the livestock drank its water and ate its grass, the range was fenced off, and no further appearances of the lady of the lake were reported. Today, only a few of the older ranchers remember the story, and those who do will say they don't believe it.

The Blue Lake Monster

THE REPORTER DIDN'T BELIEVE the story, himself, but apparently a great many people did. The editor had said, "Go up to Lake County and interview some of the eyewitnesses; there may be something to it." Like tales about talking dogs or wailing ghosts, an article concerning a frightful sea monster in a California lake would be just as hard to swallow. After all, it was 1871, and people were not as gullible as they used to be. A hideous and dangerous lake monster? Well, just maybe.

According to reports, whatever it was had been seen not once but several times in the beautiful Blue Lake just north of Clear Lake. The natives and settlers of the region had been describing the phenomenon for at least a year, and first hand accounts of such sighting were be worth a feature story.

What had made the matter newsworthy was the receipt of a letter written by a person in Lake County stating that a fabulous sea monster had been seen in the last few days. According to the correspondent, a party of picnickers from Ukiah had stopped on the shore of the lake for some kind of festival. There was a brass band present, and when it began to play, the giant fish, or whatever it was, came to the top of the water near the shore and

150

was plainly seen by all present. A member of the band had actually confirmed this report to a Healdsburg newspaper. From the description given, in size and ferocious appearance, the monster was not unlike the great dragon used by the Chinese in their New Year celebration in Chinatown.

After the necessary preparations for the journey, the reporter took passage on the little ferry that crossed the Bay and chugged its way up the Petaluma River. The wait in Petaluma was not long, and he was soon in the stagecoach headed north. His destination lay some hundred miles from San Francisco, and such a journey at best was never pleasant. It was May, and the heat of summer had already turned the grass to a scorching brown stubble; the mountain roads were steep, crooked, and always dusty; the rest stops at the inns along the way gave some relief, but the food was not of a quality to excite the palate of a true San Franciscan.

The tedium of his journey was relieved somewhat by speculation about the adventure ahead. If the strange sea monster or fresh-water creature proved genuine, there would be a story worth telling, especially if he could get a glimpse of it himself. Whether it was some kind of giant fish or a deep water mammal like the whale or a monstrous sea serpent would have to be determined. And whether it was dangerous to man was not yet clear, but certainly the natives were afraid of it. Fishermen no longer ventured out very far from shore lest their little boats might be capsized by the vicious leviathan, and the sentiment prevailed that no one could feel safe on the lake until the devilish beast was caught and disposed of.

At Ukiah he took a room at a little hotel that catered to drummers, as the more elegant traveling salesmen were called; and after settling in, he managed to talk with a few local citizens about the region and its monster. Then after a night of uncertain rest, interrupted several times by the brawling of some loggers in the saloon next door, he ventured forth to rent a horse and buggy and head for the Blue Lake, which was situated some eighteen miles northeast from Ukiah and twelve miles northwest from the town of Lakeport. His road was the main-traveled route of the stage which carried mail and passengers between these two villages. Blue Lake was situated high up in the mountains that rise, he noted on the map, between the Sacramento Valley and the upper Russian River valleys. The lake was closed in snugly on all sides by hills which were very steep; seemingly these mountainsides continued their angle of slope downward below the water until they met at a great depth below. The lake, therefore, was a very deep mountain gorge or canyon filled with water that had been sounded to a depth of three hundred feet without bottom. The water was very clear, and the reflection of the woody hills gave it a bluish tint—hence the name Blue Lake.

Following directions he had received in Ukiah he turned from the main road onto a narrow, twisting, rock-strewn dirt road that wound its way from one chuck-hole to the next around the edge of the lake. From time to time he stopped to take in the beauty of the scene. The water was motionless; the surface of the lake was like a pane of glass set in a frame of trees and jagged rocks. Could it be possible that somewhere in the deep water below, this monster fish or dragon made its home?

In Ukiah he had learned that the beast was at least thirty feet long. This had been confirmed by several of the older inhabitants of the area who had seen it from time to time during the past year. He also had been told that the Indians of that valley had long held the superstition that this giant fish was some kind of water god too powerful to offend. They never camped close to the lake. They never fished or hunted there, and they didn't care to talk about it much. Consequently, he had been told, it was unlikely that he could interview a native Indian on the subject.

There would, however, be old settlers living around the lake who would be more than willing to talk. An occasional cabin along the road confirmed the presence of such inhabitants. At last he found his man, a rustic personage of obvious antiquity who was chopping wood in his front yard near the lake. After the reporter had introduced himself and explained the purpose of his visit, the questioning began.

"First, we'll have to establish your authority on this subject. What is your name, sir?"

"Just call me Slim. My name is Wilson."

"And how long have you lived here in the vicinity of Blue Lake?"

"Oh, about twelve years. No, thirteen years now."

"And have you seen this strange fish, this sea dragon, in the lake?"

"More than once, I've seen him. But you won't see him today. He's smart. I'm goin' to catch him, though."

"You're going to catch him? Do tell! How do you plan to go about that? I take it you're not afraid of him, either?"

"Well, I wouldn't say I'm afraid, and I wouldn't say I'm not. But I'm goin' to catch him one of these days. I've got me a hook and line that'll do it. The hook is nine inches long. Kind of like a meat hook only bigger. And I've got it attached to a chain—twelve feet of chain. He's too big for any old wire, and a rope—why, he'd just bite that in two."

"What are you using for bait—or shouldn't I ask that?"

"Well, now, I'll tell you. That hook is baited with a nice big ham of venison. And it's down there right now waitin' for that fish to take hold of it."

"Yes, but what would happen if he did take hold of it? He'd just pull you in, wouldn't he?"

"Got that figured, too. That chain is fastened to a tree down there by the edge of the water. When he starts pullin' and shakin' that tree, I'll know I got him. That chain is fastened to seventy feet of big rope. I've got the double-trees all hitched to that rope, and when he's ready I'll just hitch the old team to him and pull him out. He might flop around some at first, but I aim to shoot him, and then I ought to be able to drag him out. Of course, if I could take him alive and get him in a big tank, I might take him around the country and put him in a sideshow somewhere and make some money on him, but I doubt that would be possible with what I have to work with. So I'll just shoot him."

The conversation seemed to end there, so after due thanks and a departing, "Good luck. I hope you do catch him!" the reporter climbed back into his buggy. He was beginning to sense for the first time the possible reality of the story. Wilson's confidence was strangely contagious, and the city man found himself hoping that the old-timer might indeed catch his fish.

As he continued his journey he turned his attention again to the lake, which he soon discovered to be not one but two bodies of water. The upper lake was almost cut in two by a neck of timbered land that ridged out into it leaving the waters connected by a narrow channel or neck. He noted that the upper lake was about a mile and a half long and from one-fourth to one-third of a mile wide. The lower lake, approximately half a mile south of this one, was smaller. Here indeed was a wild, rugged, and beautiful part of California to which one who loved nature at its best would want to come.

He was brought back to the mission at hand by the sudden discovery that he was in the presence of another native resident, who was sitting on a stump near the road calmly watching the approach of the stranger. He stopped, got out of his buggy, and walked toward the elfin creature, who was all the while eyeing him with obvious curiosity. When he explained that he was investigating the rumor of a lake monster, the little man on the stump broke into a broad grin.

After the preliminaries were dispensed with, the perky little man was quite willing to be interviewed. "Oh, yes," he said. "Well, me name is Michael O'Hara."

"You've lived here, how long, Mr. O'Hara?"

"Not so long. Only about five years. I'm a newcomer, as you might say, from the Old Country, as you might guess."

"Mr. O'Hara, what can you tell me about the great monster that is supposed to be in this lake?"

"Well, I heard about it a long time ago. At first I was inclined to discredit the existence of his fishship, but my doubts were dispelled the other day when I got an actual view of this curiosity myself. It was while I was comin' along the grade up there on the bank of this upper lake here—right up there, it was—last Saturday. And I hadn't been drinkin', either. I caught a glimpse of him swimming near that other shore over there. That was about four hundred yards, wouldn't you say? I stopped the team to have a good look at him. When I first saw him he was at a considerable depth in the water, but he soon rose to the surface so that I could see him plainly. You can see deeper in the water from above, you know, and I was right up there."

"I see," said the reporter. "Go on."

"Well, he moved slowly for a short distance. I was that surprised I just sat there gawkin' at him. Then he changed his direction and swam off out of sight."

"How big was this thing?"

"I should think it would measure at least twenty feet in length. And it was five or six feet around the body. May the saints believe me, he was a fearful thing. The Indians here, you know, have the superstition that a sight of this monster devil fish, as they call him, is certain death to them. But as you can see, I'm not dead yet."

"They believe that?"

"Oh, yes, they believe it. They will not fish in this lake. I refused to believe this big fish story—I've never been a superstitious type of feller—until I was convinced by seein' the evidence with my own eyes. Now I'm no longer incredulous, but I'm still not sure that I can say exactly what the creature really is. Being in the water, as it is, it is evidently a fish. But of what particular kind, your guess is as good as mine. I'm no authority on fish that are any bigger than a good-sized trout."

"What do you think of your neighbor down here, Mr. Wilson, who has set out to catch the monster?"

"Oh, that he'll never do. He's never had a bite yet, and no wonder. He never pays attention to his hook. And he never changes the bait."

The interview ended, and the reporter returned to Ukiah. He had spent a day at the lake fervently praying for the miracle of visual revelation, but unfortunately the creature had declined to show itself. As he got further away from the lake and its true believers, such as Wilson and O'Hara, his faith began to waver. Back in town he found many people who scoffed at the idea. The scales of evidence began to tilt in the direction of reason over superstition. And yet, throughout the history of the world many obviously sane and sensible people had reported witnessing incredible phenomena which later turned out to be real. No doubt a hundred years hence there would still be accounts of strange and unearthly forms of life witnessed by honest and sincere observers.

Perhaps in this truth lay the real story—that it is natural for mankind to see things that cannot be measured, believe things that cannot be proved, and fish for things that cannot be caught.

The Bucking Bear of Bodega

I CAN'T TELL this story in Ace Morgan's exact words. He was a champion storyteller, and it wouldn't do to try to imitate him, but I can remember most of it. They say that truth can be stranger than fiction, and this time I guess it is; the story even got into the history books, and that ought to make it more or less true. So you can believe it if you want to. Anyway, it won't take long and it won't hurt much.

Back in 1852 the lumber mills in and around Bodega in Sonoma County were doing pretty well. The loggers were busy in the woods, and the mill hands had to hustle to keep the logs going in and the lumber coming out. Men drifted in and drifted out like fleas jumping from one dog to another. But there were always a few steady hands who stayed on and got to be pretty well known around the place.

The little town of Bodega was proud and lively then. There were boarding houses and hotels, and plenty of saloons to provide the higher necessities of life. Every once in awhile the old town would get itself wound up for a fight, and then things really would break loose. Sometimes there would be a dozen fights in one night.

Next day you could see plenty of broken noses, black eyes, and bruised fists—and even a few stitches here and there on various parts of sundry anatomies. But that kind of ruckus was more or less normal.

It was also normal for a man like "Jersey" Roy to have enemies in a place like that. Nobody knows what his last name was, but they called him "Jersey" because that's where he said he came from, New Jersey. He was a gambler who played his cards close to his vest. Some said he had nimble fingers, but maybe that was only because he won most of the time. He was doing pretty well for himself there in Bodega and was piling up a sizeable stake, to judge from the way he was always taking in money and not paying out much.

It was natural, therefore, that he should have some unfriendly acquaintances. Now, not all of a gambler's enemies are going to be the loud-mouthed, table-slapping, hard-drinking big losers. There are also the hard cases that hover close to the bar to pick up free drinks and nurse secret wounds. Maybe life has kicked them where it hurts, and they have settled down like a dog in a corner privately hating anyone who is successful.

And there are also the slick, slithery ones. They think they are clever, and never pass up a chance to play an angle of some sort. They like to turn men against each other and then slip in and steal the pieces. They are cowards at heart and hate themselves for it.

That kind of man was Tony West. He worked at the mill on the early shift. Afternoons and evenings he was always hanging around the card tables, and particularly he attached himself to "Jersey." Then it got so they were taking their meals together. And finally it came out that they were staying at the same boarding house. You could figure that West was up to something.

There was another kind, too, that you could find around the mill towns. Fellows like Andy Stump. Andy worked hard and kept out of trouble. He was always good for a laugh and was well liked by everybody.

These are the three men in our story—"Jersey" Roy, Tony West, and Andy Stump. We haven't got to the bear yet. Well, one day in the fall of 1852, "Jersey" failed to show up for lunch. He always got up late, and nobody expected him for breakfast. But at lunch he was missed. That night, people began to inquire about him. He had disappeared.

Tony West said that "Jersey" had packed up and pulled out for San Francisco, leaving the money with him to pay the board bill. Nobody cared much, but people thought it was pretty strange behavior. Of course, if Tony West had done him in they might have a good lynching party. But nobody got very excited about it.

Well, a couple of days later, West got into some kind of ruckus with Andy Stump. Nobody remembered much what it was all about, but those two boys got mad and threw hot words at each other. They were standing by a pile of logs out near the edge of the clearing not far from the woods, and they were just about to tear into each other. Andy looked around to see if he could lay his hands on a cant hook or a good hand-sized limb, just to use for emphasis, you understand. There wasn't anything like that around, so Andy decided to go to work on West with his fists. As Andy came close he felt the impulse to bestow on West a few well-chosen words as a kind of psychological attack before the real onslaught. He let go with a barrage of language such as only a Missouri mule could fully comprehend or appreciate, and then for a climax he accused Tony West of murdering "Jersey" Roy. He came right out and said it. "You murderin', thievin' rat. You killed Jersey and left him layin' out there in the woods somewhere. And now I'm goin' to do the same for you, you low-down skunk!" Andy came rushing in to make good his threat.

But something suddenly came over Tony West. The direct accusation of murder was a surprise. He turned pale. He backed away, trying to think. Andy must know the truth. The other mill hands standing around must also know the truth. He had better get out of there fast.

West turned and ran into the brush. This was his admission of guilt. Everybody now knew that he had murdered "Jersey." So all the mill hands joined in the chase, with Andy Stump in the lead. Between some piles of lumber and around a pile of redwood logs they ran. Off into the thick shrubbery and down the canyon darted West, with Andy close behind and the other mill hands trailing after.

West was a good runner, but Andy was equal to him. He was chasing a murderer now, and sweet vengeance was just within Andy's reach. The other mill hands were soon left trailing far behind. West zig-zagged down a dark, steep ravine, evidently expecting to find a hiding place in the tangled undergrowth and vines.

As the two reached a small clearing, with only a few yards between them now, West leaped over a bank near a creek bed. In the brush on the other side he stumbled over something alive. It was a cub bear. The surprised cub let out a howl of fright and pain, and so did West. The little bear scampered off, and West got to his feet and ran on.

Andy tried to stop when he saw the bear, but the hillside was too steep and he was going too fast. He jumped the creek and went crashing and floundering down through the vines and saplings on the other side. He made another mighty jump and landed on something that was just as alive and moving as the cub had been. To his terrible surprise he found himself squarely on the back of the old mama grizzly bear.

The old bear had seen West fall over her cub, and she regarded him as the enemy. She was just beginning to chase the assailant of her offspring when Andy came down on her back. This added blow infuriated her, and snorting with anger she bounded after West for all she was worth.

Poor Andy grabbed himself two big fists full of hair and held on. He didn't dare let go for fear she would turn on him. Anyway she was going so fast he was afraid that if he did let go he would dash his brains out against a tree or a rock. Or maybe he was just too scared to do anything but hang on for dear life.

That was a chase the likes of which had never been seen before in the redwood country, and would never be seen again. The three of them crashed through the woods, with West running for his life—clothing torn and disarranged, his body scratched and bleeding—and the bear snorting fire with every leap, and there rode Stump also with clothes torn, hair flying, face and arms cut and scratched, but pulling bear hair for all he was worth.

Stump weighed one hundred seventy-three pounds. This extra weight slowed the bear down, and West began to pull ahead in the race. About that time the bear passed a point where the stream below them looked fairly deep. It was now or never for Andy. He let go of the bear and took a dive into a pool of water about eighteen feet below the trail. He swam underwater across the creek and came up behind some overhanging branches on the other side. He could hear the old she-bear still crashing through the brush. So after he had rested and felt safe again he crawled out and limped back to the mill. The story he had to tell was hard to believe, but Andy's condition was pretty good proof that it was true.

The next day a searching party went out and picked up the trail. And when they returned they reported that Andy Stump's tale was true. After Andy and the bear had parted company, she had gone on chasing West and picking up speed with every jump. Not far down the hill she had caught him. And that old grizzly bear had killed him pretty quickly, you can bet on that. She had chewed him up considerably, too, around the head and neck.

After a little more searching, the party had also found the body of "Jersey" Roy. He had been murdered, all right. His throat had been cut, evidently with a keen-edge knife. Apparently West had killed him and hidden the body in the very same part of the wood where he ran so frantically to save his own life.

So there you have it. Will Rogers once said something like, "California is a hard state to lie about; no matter what you tell, it might be true." So if anybody doubts anything you say about California from now on, just remember this story of how, in 1852 in the town of Bodega, a full-grown man took a bareback ride on a bear's back, and how that grizzly bear captured, prosecuted, convicted, and executed a murderer. Ace Morgan even swore that the bear was so popular after that spectacular punishment of crime that she was elected justice of the peace and held office for two years. But I doubt that.

The Legend of Charlie Hanes

I THINK IT WAS Mark Twain who once said, "The truth is such a rare commodity that we should be sparing in the use of it." I think it was Mark Twain. Anyway, in spite of my truth-loving Quaker ancestry I can enjoy a little exaggeration once in awhile. Seems like it's just human nature to exaggerate a little. It puts me in mind of a pretty good example of this sort of thing. It was up in the big redwoods, and there was a little logging camp way back in the hills. The men ran out of food so they drew lots and sent one of the fellows down to the settlement for supplies.

He drove off in the wagon, and after a couple of days he was back. His wagon was loaded with supplies, all right. When the loggers went out to help him unpack they looked in the wagon and found thirty-two cases of whiskey and three loaves of bread. One of the loggers scratched his head and said, "Say, now! What are we goin' to do with all this bread?" Now that illustrates my point. There is a little exaggeration in this story. The truth was that there was only one loaf of bread, not three.

And this brings me to one of the best yarn-spinners I ever knew. That was old Charlie Hanes. He's been dead a long time, now. But he used to brag that folks called him the biggest liar in

Colusa County. I've had him as a guest on radio and television, and some of his stories have been recorded for the Library of Congress. This is his story, every word of it, just as he told it to me.

I

Well, now get ready for the big one. I'll be glad to tell that story because, you know, that really happened—that story. I lived up at Stony Ford in a little white house next to the Catholic Church. I had four children at that time, and I was havin' a hard time makin' a living, getting a dollar and a half a day, you know. So I said to myself—I just sat down and said to myself, "Charlie, you gotta do something, that's all, or the family's goin' to starve to death." So I went out—I'll tell you what I done: I went out and bought two hundred turkey hens, you see, and I bought me nine toms, and that year I hatched off the most wonderful hatch of turkeys that you ever saw. Twenty-one birds to a hen, and that's a good hatch. You know, that's over a hundred percent increase.

Well, I raised them birds up till they was about half growed, you know, and I went out to Colusa—right south of Colusa—and I rented a stubble field, forty acres of barley and wheat stubble. I put me up a tent there, and I brought my turkeys out there. But I had no gun with me, not a thing to do any hunting with.

There was this big pond—oh, the most beautiful lake you ever saw, just washed out from the river there, you know. It was a good sized one, I'll tell you, boy. And every day there'd be thousands of geese coming in there and land on that lake, and no way for me to get 'em. And I wanted to get some of them geese so bad to send up on the stage for my folks. I knew my kids were just dying to get some of them geese. But I didn't have a gun, and I didn't know what I was goin' to do.

So one day I was thinking, and I thought I'll just try this little scheme on 'em. So I went down there one morning, and I just stepped around that lake. Oh, it was quite a distance around it. I stepped it up to an old dead tree there, you know. And then I went downtown and bought enough rope to go clear around that lake. I laid the rope clear around the lake and up behind this tree, and I sat down there waitin' for 'em. I tied a loop in the rope, made it like a kind of a big noose, you see, around that lake.

Pretty soon here come thousands of geese—thousands of 'em— come down and set right down in that water, you know. And I pulled up on that old rope and caught 'em by the legs. And I thought, I've got 'em now. But I forgot to tie the rope; I was just a-holdin' it there. And the first thing I knew they all took off— started to fly away, and me holding the rope. Why, first thing I knew I was seventeen feet up in the air. Yeah! I just never tied the rope, and I didn't let go till it was too late, and they were flyin' away with me. They got way up in the air, and they circled three or four times with me up there, and headed straight west for Stony Ford. Yeah, Stony Ford.

Yes, sir. I said to myself, "I wonder where they're goin' with me now. Ahhh, they're goin' over that dam—that big dam over there at Stony Ford—and they're gonna drown me." Well, sir, they went over there and they flew right over the top of that dam, brother, and they never stopped. They just went right straight on. And I said to myself, I said, "I wonder where they're goin' with me now. I bet they're taking me to the ocean, that's where they're going. Charlie, they're takin' you to the ocean to drown you!"

And then they went right over my house. Right over my house! I looked down—oh, I was up there quite a ways—I was thinkin' of my folks. "Oh, I hope I can see my kids once more." I was sailin' up in the air quite a ways, and I looked down and could see my kids out there in the yard playing. Just having a big time. Well, a couple of them got in a fight, and my wife come out and give one of 'em a paddling for fighting, so that made me mad. But I thought about the geese, so I pulled myself up the rope just as fast as I could and I jerked out seven geese and wrung their heads off and throwed 'em down to the kids. And I said, "They'll have something to eat, anyway." And I bid them all goodbye. I said, "Goodbye, kids. You'll never see your daddy again. He's goin' to be dropped in the ocean and be drownded!"

They were headin' straight for Snow Mountain, goin' right to the ocean. They went over that first little range of hills, and on to where old Fouts Springs was, you know, and old Wagstaff, the old cook, he was out in the yard. I hollered, "Goodbye, Wag. You're never gonna see Charlie no more, that's all. He's goin' to the ocean to get drownded."

And then we went right over the top of old Snow Mountain. I'll tell you, that mountain is seven thousand feet high. I said, "I hope this rope's long enough to reach the ground. That's my last chance." But it looked like I was up too high. It looked like I was seventy-five feet in the air. Well, sir, pretty soon I saw something comin' at me, and it looked like a big stove pipe. It kept gettin' bigger and bigger and bigger and bigger, you know.

And then I could see that it was a big pine tree standing up there seventy-five feet high with the top broke off. Well, the rope went by that tree, and I let loose of the rope and let 'em go. I landed right on top of that tree. The whole top was gone, and that tree was holler. Down that holler I went, clear to the bottom of that tree, seventy-five feet. Oh, I like to of tore my clothes off goin' down inside there. Well, there I was down at the bottom of that tree lookin' up through that little round hole. Why, man, I was wondering how I was ever goin' to get out.

Well, I got my old pocket knife out. I've got it right here in my pocket. See? And I said, "Charlie, you're gonna have to wear this knife out cutting out of here. You'll starve to death before you get out of this tree." And pretty soon something touched against my leg. Wow! Something was in there alive with me! I reached down. I felt around slowly, like this, see, and my hand settled in some fur down there. Fur! "Oh, wow!" I said to myself. "That's some kind of an animal!"

Oh, man, it was dark in there and I couldn't see. So I reached in my pocket and hunted up a match. I lit that match, and there was two little cub bears layin' in there. The cutest things I ever saw. They wasn't over that long. "Aiee, aiee!" I said to myself. "I'll eat them bears before I ever get out of here. I'll live several days off them while I'm cutting my way out." So I just sat down there, and one got on one knee and the other got on the other knee, and I was just havin' a lot of fun with those little bears, there.

Well, I sat there about thirty minutes, I guess, and pretty soon something hit me on the head, and all at once it got awful dark in there. I looked up that hole, and here come that old mother bear, backin' down to me. Down that hole! Then I knew I was done for. "Wow!" I said to myself, "Charlie, now you're a goner. She'll feed you to these cubs instead of you eatin' them." So she got down close to me, and I happened to think of my knife. (Here, look at that knife. That's a long, slim blade. See it?)

I stood right there waitin' for that old baby. I said, "Listen, old sweetheart, you're gonna get in trouble when you get down here." When she got down there where I could reach her, I just grabbed her by the leg and I soused that knife into her bottom. Wow! She went right up that tree with me hangin' on. Took me straight up there like nobody's business. You never seen anything go up a tree as fast as she went up that tree, and me draggin' on to her. She got almost to the top, there, and she slipped. She started falling—came back about ten feet—and I give her another souse with the knife, and she went right up to the top.

When she got on top I grabbed the top of the tree, and I rammed that knife into her, and she just let all holds loose and hit the ground on her back. She rolled down that hill—oh, she must have rolled sixty yards, I guess. Well, I was comin' down that tall tree just as fast as I could come down. I figured she would be ready for me. Well, I got down to about ten or fifteen feet off the ground, and here she come up that hill after me. Oh, she was buckin' up that hill after me, fellers, I'll tell you! And I was on this side of the tree and she was on the other side, and we ducked around there awhile, and pretty soon she come around after me and I kicked her right in the chest. Oh, I give her a good jar, you know, and knocked her over.

She rolled down the hill again twenty or thirty yards, and I come down out of that tree as fast as I could and hit the ground. Well, she tore after me, and I went down that steep mountain lickety-split. Boy, I'll tell you right now, I was a fast runner but that old bear was just grabbin' for me every jump I made. Well, I zig-zagged down there about half a mile at top speed, and I could feel her breath on me all the way.

She was just about to get me, and there was a big rock standing right ahead. I said to myself, "I'll fool her." And all at once I jumped to one side right quick, see, and that old bear just slid right on past me. About ten or fifteen feet—I didn't watch to see how far she went, for sure. I run around behind that rock and hid from her.

Well, there was a little canyon right there, and I run over there as fast as I could go, and I took off down that canyon just as hard as I could run. I went on down to Fouts Springs and had supper with old Wagstaff. I went on over and stayed all night with my folks. And the next day I went back over to Colusa. It took me two days to round up all my turkeys. They were scattered all over the country.

II

Now you want me to tell you the one about the big snake? Well, Mark Sisk and me, we were working for Casserine over on the Little Stony, and one day he said, "Boys, I want you to go down to that field by the river and shock up that forty acres of hay that's been cut and laying there." And he said, "It's already in the windrows, so just shock it up, and then bring a load back with you when you get through."

So we took the hay wagon and went down there to shock up the hay. We worked for a couple of hours and it was gettin' pretty hot by then, so I decided to get me a smoke and have a little rest. There was a big mush oak standing over there with some good shade so I got out my Durham tobacco—I always rolled 'em out of Durham tobacco, you know—and I got this tobacco out and the pitchfork under my arm, and I walked over to this big mush oak tree there, you know. And the grass was about two foot high. Two or three feet high, maybe, under that tree. So I walked right up there, not lookin' too close at anything.

Well, there lay a big snake in there—about fourteen feet long he was, as I remember, and just layin' there. And I guess about a foot and a half around him. So I took him for a big limb that fell out of this tree, you know—just grass all around, and me not lookin' too close.

Well, sir, I just turned around and sat down right in the middle of that big snake. Man! He just throwed me right over backwards—like that! Lost my tobacco and fork, you know—fork went one way and the 'baccer went another. And I saw that big snake, and he was a-comin' at me—standin' four feet high and lickin' his tongue out at me!

So I grabbed up the fork and I was a-goin' to kill him. and then I thought better of it. I said to myself, "Charlie, if you can catch that snake—" I said, "If I can catch you, brother, I'll put you in a tent show and charge two bits for people just to come in and look at you. Why, Charlie, you got a fortune." So I just stood there. I didn't kill him.

Well, that old snake just made a big jump at me—and he was comin' at me, see. And so I grabbed up the fork and I shoved that fork handle at him and stopped him. You know, that fella swallowed that fork handle right up to the tongs! Then he got ready to plunge at me, and he hit me in the stomach, and I jumped back, and he made another plunge. Didn't hit me quite as hard but it was heavy enough.

So I started running for the wagon, and that snake just awhippin' me all the way down there. So when I got to the wagon I made a big leap up on that flat wagon, and that old snake he just throwed the last half of me on. Well, that snake couldn't get at me then, and I'd run around this way and that way, see; and that old snake, he was running around. Wherever I went, he was there. And pretty soon he got mad, and he run over there and shoved that fork into a big shock of hay. Well, sir, he picked it up and threw that hay at me. Yes, he did! And, boy! He run and grabbed another and throwed it at me. And another! "Wow!" I said. "I'll just load this wagon."

So I commenced to kick that hay around and load the wagon. And that old snake was just pickin' up that hay and throwin' it at me. And he loaded that whole wagon. I'll bet you in a half an hour's time he had two ton of hay on that wagon. Load hay? Why, man, I never saw anything like it. I was afraid he was goin' to break the wagon down, so I hollered, "Mark, come on, let's get out of here!" And I reached down and grabbed the lines and out of there we went. I looked back and I could see him runnin' around with that hay.

So we went home, and the next morning I got me a new fork and I come back over there. We did! And you know, that snake had shocked up that forty acres of hay, and was standin' there on the bank of the creek giggin' himself a mess of suckers for his breakfast.

Big Foot Strides Again

THE STRANGE CREATURE must weigh over six hundred pounds. It walks upright like a man, but its arms are long and ape-like and its body is completely covered with hair—except for its face, which is smooth and brown. The face is flat and round, the nose is flat, the ears are small. The eyes are round and expressionless. If the face shows any feeling at all, it might be described as a kind of bewildered loneliness.

This huge, melancholy creature stalks through the forests of northern California leaving footprints that are sixteen inches long, with marks of big human toes. It walks like a man, and when it runs the strides are ten feet long. Its hands are those of a man, and the handprints measure eleven inches from the wrist to the tip of the fingers. This humanoid creature, this man-like animal or animal-like giant man is reported from time to time—not from footprints alone, like the abominable snowman, but from face-to-face encounters—and there are people who swear to it. This is Big Foot—gigantic, harmless, forlorn, half-human Big Foot, who hides somewhere in the wild mountains of northern California.

The brute presumably has been seen by hikers and fishermen, searched for by expeditions, allegedly photographed, and even cast as a character in television "documentaries." Yet he or she has never been captured. Many people have claimed some kind of contact with such a creature, enough to give credence to the existence of this legendary giant. The stories are more convincing because all the informants from different times and places agree on the basic facts. One of the most intimate encounters with Big Foot comes from an interview in 1963 with Mr. and Mrs. C.A. Jenkins of Fort Bragg.

On February 16, 1962, Big Foot or something resembling Big Foot appeared to them in person. It was a cold rainy morning. A heavy fog had come in from the coast to the foothills behind Fort Bragg, and now at about a quarter to five the rain was beginning to cut through the fog and melt it down for a bleak, soggy, sunless dawn. Outside the Jenkins' place the dogs were barking. Bob Hatfield, the brother of Mrs. Jenkins and a boarder in the house, got up and went outside to see what was the matter. A six-foot solid board fence stood between the yard and the forest beyond. As Hatfield came close to the fence, where the agitated dogs stood, he was able to make out through the half darkness a huge figure towering above the fence and apparently looking down at the dogs.

Hatfield came back to the house and awakened Jenkins and his wife. "Come on out," he said, "and I'll show you the biggest bear you'll ever see." So Jenkins got up and walked out with him. The creature was not by the fence where it had been before, and it was still too dark to see the rest of the yard clearly. Jenkins turned and went back to the house to get a flashlight and a gun. His thought was to look around the yard to see if the bear had climbed in, or to search beyond the high fence to see if he could locate the animal in the forest beyond and perhaps get a shot at him. He was in the house several minutes looking for shells for the gun. His wife was getting dressed. Outside, Hatfield went to the other side of the house and looked out toward the brush. He couldn't see anything.

But just at that moment the great beast stepped over a little two-foot garden fence near the house and loomed up in the darkness almost beside Hatfield. The man screamed, terrified by the suddenness of it, and jumped back. He stumbled and fell. Jenkins, inside the house, heard the scream. Thinking the animal had attacked his brother-in-law, he came running to the window and looked out. He could see the large hairy body standing by the window. Hatfield came crawling through the door, which Mrs. Jenkins held open for him. When she tried to close the door it wouldn't shut. Something was pushing against it from the outside holding it two or three inches open. She yelled to Jenkins, "Hurry up with that gun—it's coming through the door!"

Jenkins, now ready with his gun, said, "Well, let it in, and I'll get it."

But the thing did not push the door any further open; it stepped back and stood looking at the half open door and the people inside. Jenkins went to the window again and looked out into the half darkness. He could see it standing back a step or two from the door. As he watched, it turned and walked away. It moved slowly toward the driveway about fifty feet away, stepped over the two-foot fence again, and walked on out the driveway and off into the darkness.

Thinking on it afterward, they remembered that while the creature was standing by the doorway they had smelled a strange and terrible odor. They waited until daylight and then went outside to look around. The monster had gone, but they found one big footprint — smeared and not clearly distinguishable, but they thought it was a footprint. As they came back to the house Mrs. Jenkins noticed a hand print on the side of the wall by the door. It was immense. She got her tape measure and went back out and measured it. The print was exactly eleven and a half inches from the wrist to the tip of the finger. Obviously that was too large to be the print of a human hand, yet there it was, palm, fingers, and all.

The Jenkinses did not see the creature again. However, a man who owned a ranch about twenty miles up into the woods from their place reported seeing the same thing a few days later. His description of it was the same. Hatfield, who stood face-to-face with it and got the best look at it, described the monster as being very large, the body all covered with hair, the arms long. The face was flat; the eyes were round and dull in appearance.

Mrs. Jenkins explained, "At the time we didn't know what it was, and naturally we were startled and frightened. We were really frightened. But since then we have heard different stories about this thing. If it had wanted to come through the door that night and harm us it could have. I think it was more curious than anything else, because it didn't offer to come in. There was no sound from it at all. So I don't think it would harm us even if we saw it in broad daylight. I don't think it would."

That fitted the common description of Big Foot. The Jenkinses never did say that they thought it was Big Foot; they never would say what they thought it was, except that it definitely was not a bear, nor was it a man. But their experience corresponds with those of others who have described a similar monster. It has been called by many names, a "Yetti," a "Saskatchie," a "Sasquatch," an ape man, a wild man, and Big Foot.

Stories about such a gigantic wild man roaming these northern mountains appeared in the news during the Gold Rush days. Indians were said to have described such a creature as early as the 1840s. In 1890 an occurrence was reported in Oregon, when such a large wild man came into a logging camp, stole food, ransacked the camp, and left footprints of great size. But there is no proof that this was true.

In 1901 a timber cruiser named Mike King working in British Columbia reported an experience he had with what he called a "monkey man of the forest." It was late in the afternoon when he saw the huge man-beast standing over a water hole washing some moose meat that he was placing in two great piles. When he saw King the creature gave a startled cry and ran up the hillside. He stopped some distance away and stood watching King. He was covered with reddish brown hair, and his arms were peculiarly long and were used freely in climbing and brush running. His tracks showed a distinct human foot with very long toes.

It is said that the Indians in some parts of British Columbia are quite familiar with this ape-man. One Indian family, a Mr. and Mrs. Chapman, lived with their four children on a small farm on the Fraser River in 1941. The man was working with the railroad. His children were playing in the field, and the oldest child saw what he thought was a very large bear coming out of the woods. As the thing came closer, Mrs. Chapman saw that it was not a bear at all, but a gigantic human-like monster covered with hair. It went into the Chapman house and carried out a fifty-gallon barrel of salt fish, broke it open, and scattered the fish around the yard. She guessed it to be about seven or eight feet tall. Although it did not offer to harm the children it did seem to be very hungry. Having taken what fish it wanted, it disappeared into the woods.

In August, 1958, a tractor driver named Jerry Croon was working with a road crew cutting a road through a forest in Humboldt County. One morning when he went to start his tractor he saw a series of large footprints around the machine. They looked to be over sixteen inches long. He and his boss followed the tracks, which led to the storage area for the project. A 55-gallon drum of diesel fuel was missing. They followed the footprints to the edge of a steep ravine. Lying at the bottom of the hill was the missing drum; it had been carried sixty yards to the edge and had been thrown over and had rolled the rest of the way down.

Professional hunters were called in to track the guilty beast. They easily picked up the tracks around the camp and followed for some distance. Suddenly as they looked ahead they saw what seemed to be a gigantic human covered with brown hair and squatting near the road. It sprang up and crossed the road in two strides and vanished through the undergrowth. Four dogs were sent into the brush after it. From time to time they were heard barking, each time further away. Then the barking stopped. The dogs never returned.

In recent years the tracks of Big Foot have been reported in Humboldt, Siskiyou, Plumas, and Mendocino counties. They are always the same—more human than animal and very large. Whether there is more than one such monster no one knows. Old hunters who speculate on these matters say there could easily be several, male and female. After all, unless their life span is miraculously long, it must logically follow that there is some natural means of reproduction. There are vast wilderness areas in northern California where a whole colony could exist for years without being detected.

Apparently this legendary beast is harmless. Big and strong enough to crush a man with a single blow, the thing seems to be as afraid of people as they are of him. He gets hungry and comes out looking for food. He gets lonely, or curious, and comes out to look at people and their strange manner of life. It was reported that the one seen by Jenkins and Hatfield was a female, but Mr. Jenkins says that was only a rumor he started as a joke. "My brother-in-law was a bachelor, you see," he chuckled, "and I told him I thought the thing must have been a female out looking for a mate, and Bob was it." Such family gossip, of course, was not intended for publication.

However, in all sincerity Mr. and Mrs. Jenkins insist that they did actually see the monster, and they frightened it away. But others in the same community say the monster exists only in imagination, that it is a hoax revived from time to time for publicity or notoriety. And this has been proved true of many instances of "sightings" of Big Foot.

No matter who is right, it is safe to predict that Big Foot will be reported again somewhere in the wilds of northern California. He will appear, a lonely wanderer leaving his giant footprints behind for people to wonder at and speculate about. He will never be killed or captured but will continue to live on, a sad and lonely, flat-faced, round-eyed, hairy, frightful thing with an unpleasant odor. And his legend, like his footprints, will continue to grow.

III. BEHIND THE SCENES

BEHIND THE SCENES

A legend usually becomes more interesting when we know a little about what went on behind the scenes either in the origin of the story or the published studies about it. No attempt is made here to note all the scholarship about any story, but the student of California legendry can easily backtrack these references to other sources if he wishes.

The folklorist likes to refer to catalogued tale types and motifs found in narrative lore; consequently, when they are applicable these index numbers have been listed here. For example, the tall tale of Charlie Hanes is listed in Antti Aarne and Stith Thompson, *The Types of the Folktale* (Helsinki: FF Communications No. 3, 1961), as "Man carried through the air by geese" (Type 1881). And the motifs or narrative elements within the tale are identified by number as indexed by Ernest Baughman, *Type and Motif Index of the Folklore of England and North America* (Indiana University Folklore Series No. 20, 1966); for example, "Boy falls into hollow stump with bear cubs" (X1133.1). When such notations occur in this section, therefore, they refer to the tale type or motif listed in these reference works.

Unpublished material may be found in the folklore archives cited in the libraries at Sonoma State University and California State University, Chico, and at the Folklore and Mythology Center at the University of California, Los Angeles.

SNOWSHOE THOMPSON

The physical stamina and almost superhuman endurance of Snowshoe Thompson, combined with his unselfish commitment to a worthy cause, have made him a truly legendary figure in California history. In some quarters he is still considered a patron saint of skiers in the West, and at Boreal Ridge there is a small museum for exhibiting his memorabilia. As is characteristic of the legend, his story is a cluster of anecdotes in which the details and presumed facts vary according to the version.

In the present text, for instance, the episode of the wolves is factually suspect. It is unlikely that there were timber wolves in the region. But someone somewhere did have the experience, and the dramatic situation has survived by attaching itself to the Thompson cycle. Such is the accretional characteristic of legendary figures.

An early version of the Thompson story was told by Dan de Quille (William Wright) in "Snow-Shoe Thompson," *Overland Monthly*, VIII, No. 46 (October, 1886), 419-435. See also George Wharton James, *Heroes of California* (Boston: Little, Brown & Company, 1910); and also Mildred B. Hoover, H.E. Rensch, and E.G. Rensch, *Historic Spots in California* (Stanford: Stanford University Press, 1932, 1962).

JOSEPH CHAPMAN, EL INGLÉS

The story of Joseph Chapman is not widely known in California today except to students of history. But among the descendants of those First Families of California who bore such names as Arriaga, Carrillo, Feliz, Sepulveda, Vallejo, and Ortega, the legend still lives. For many, José Chapman was an ancestor, and his story is part of a noble family heritage. The details of the legend may vary with the version told, but the essential facts are retained in the saga.

Some historians say that Chapman was California's first American (in 1818). Others give that honor to John Gilroy (1814) or Thomas Doak (1816). References: S.C. Foster, "José Chapman," *History of Santa Barbara and Ventura Counties* (Berkeley: Howell-North, 1961, a reproduction edition); Lola B. Hoffman, *California's Beginnings* (Sacramento: California State Publishing Co., 1948); Feliz Risenbert, *The Golden Road* (New York: McGraw Hill, 1962); Fr. Zephyrin Engelhardt, *Santa Barbara Mission* (San Francisco: The James H. Barry Co., 1923); Southern California Writers' Project, Santa Barbara, *A Guide to the Channel City and Its Environs* (New York: Hastings House Publishers, 1941); Charles E. Chapman *A History of California: The Spanish Period* (New York: Macmillan, 1921); Ralph J. Roske, *Everyman's Eden* (New York: Macmillan, 1968).

CHARLEY PARKHURST

Charley Parkhurst is one of California's legendary figures. That he was really a woman was probably not as well kept a secret as the folk like to think. The truth must have been known, at least to the other drivers and the employers, but apparently they held their tongues out of respect for the remarkable Charley. Certainly his gender could not have been widely known because, if the records are correct, he voted in 1868; this made him the first woman in the United States to vote in a national election.

Charley lies buried in the Watsonville Pioneer Cemetery, where the Pajaro Valley Historical Society erected a monument bearing the following inscription: "Charley Darkey Parkhurst, 1812-1879. Noted whip of the Gold Rush Days. Drove stage over Mt. Madonna in early days of Valley. Last run, San Juan to Santa Cruz. Death in cabin near 7-mile house. Revealed 'One-Eyed Charley' a woman. The first woman to vote in the U.S., Nov. 3, 1868."

For background reading see: Doris E. Tull, "The Coachman Was a Lady," *San Francisco Chronicle*, June 3, 1966; Mary Chaney Hoffman, "Whips of the Old West," *The American Mercury*, April, 1957; Howard Watkins, "One-Eyed Charlie's Secret," *Westways*, October, 1960; John V. Young, "The Woman Who Fooled the West," *The New York Times*, November 2, 1969. On stagecoaching in California see Helene Bacon Boggs, *My Playhouse Was a Concord Coach* (Oakland, California: Privately Printed, 1942).

THE CASE OF VALLEJO *vs.* EL AZUCARERO

Hoaxes make good folklore. People particularly like to tell about how a clever con artist outwits a person who should know better. In California, one of the most famous hoaxes was pulled on the brilliant San Francisco financier William Ralston and some of the world's greatest financial wizards when two old prospectors sold them a non-existent diamond mine. See David Lavender, *Nothing Seemed Impossible* (Palo Alto: American West Pub. Co., 1975); or Hector Lee, "Diamonds from the Big Rock Candy Mountain," *Tales of California*.

General Mariano Vallejo, a legendary figure in northern California, was commander of the Mexican northern outpost at Sonoma when in 1846 the Bear Flag Revolt snatched that part of the region from Mexico. His image is that of a wise and generous patron saint, too clever to be duped—except by his own fantasies.

JUANITA

Although this episode in California history has been recounted in various pamphlets not readily available, the version told here closely follows the earliest and more or less official source: Fariss and Smith, *History of Plumas, Lassen & Sierra Counties, California, 1882,* [Reproduced by Howell-North Books, 1971] pp. 445-447. This source includes the George Barton poem, which was much longer than the excerpt printed here.

The Fourth of July speaker imported from Sacramento was Judge John

B. Weller, who later became Governor. The second speaker was probably a local butcher named Hogue, who was said to be a spellbinding orator, particularly on political subjects. A man named Galloway was elected Justice of the Peace in 1851, and it is quite possible that it was he who presided at the trial, though there seems to be no direct evidence of this. Fariss and Smith name V.C. McMurry as the companion of Jack Cannon and the only eyewitness to the killing who gave testimony.

The story of Juanita is not widely known in California, but it has lingered as a local legend in the northern Sierra country.

KISSANE

The story of Kissane is another of California's regional legends. It is, however, an example of a family saga that is both local history and family tradition. Temelec Hall after several years of neglect and disintegration was purchased by E.D. Coblentz, who was the editor of *The San Francisco Call Bulletin*, a popular Hearst paper. Mr. and Mrs. Coblentz restored the mansion and grounds and made the place once again an elegant country home. Noted travelers—royalty, statesmen, scientists, writers, theatrical stars—from all over the world were entertained there.

It was Mr. Coblentz who first compiled the facts from which this version of the story is told. He published the account in a small privately printed pamphlet for his family and friends.

Ultimately the mansion and lands of Temelec were purchased by a group who made the place into an adult retirement community. Temelec Hall became a clubhouse for the residents of the community and is now designated as California Historical Site No. 237. Its story has been told more recently (1967) by Mrs. Lillian M. Wilson in a privately published pamphlet, *Temelec Hall Saga*.

For the full story of the Walker adventure in Nicaragua see David I. Folkman, *The Nicaragua Route* (Salt Lake City: University of Utah Press, 1972).

PETER LASSEN

For the historical facts behind the legend of Peter Lassen, see the following: Richard Dillon, *Humbugs and Heroes: A Gallery of California Pioneers* (Garden City: Doubleday and Company, 1970); Philip Ferry, "He Left a Name," *Westways* (Los Angeles: Automobile Club of Southern California, February, 1949); W.H. Hutchinson, "Lassen County's War of Independence," *Westways* (March, 1951); Aubrey Neasham, *Peter Lassen* (San Francisco: Fandango Press Book Club of California Keepsakes Series No. 42, 1979); Franklin D. Scott, "Peter Lassen, Danish Pioneer of

California," *Southern California Quarterly* (Summer, 1981); Ruby Swartzlow, "Peter Lassen, Northern California's Trail Blazer," *California Historical Quarterly* (December, 1939); Ruby Swartzlow, *Lassen: His Life and Legacy* (Mineral: Loomis Museum Association, 1964).

LIEUTENANT BEALE AND HIS CAMELS

Ghost camels haunting the western American deserts make good folklore. The short-lived plan to hold annual camel races at Virginia City, on the other hand, did not become a folk tradition; they belong more to commercial promotion than the folk, and are therefore not folklore. Old Hi Jolly was real, however, and Lieutenant Beale's camels are a part of California's history. For the story, complete with a good bibliography, see Odie B. Falk, *The U.S. Camel Corps* (New York: Oxford University Press, 1976).

A QUESTION OF MARRIAGE

Anyone working in matters of family relationships sooner or later encounters the traditional attitudes and codes of the family itself. If it happens to be a family that helped to make history—such as the Lees of Virginia, the Youngs of Utah, the Sepulvedas or the Carrillos of California—the traditional family image is usually reinforced by legends which glorify or in some way memorialize a colorful ancestor.

This is such a family legend. It comes from the folklore archives of Sonoma State University as well as from actual history and is accepted as true by the descendants of the families involved. That it is also a love story makes it even more acceptable as a carrier of tradition.

HOW TO DISSOLVE A PARTNERSHIP

The fight between Dawson and McIntosh is indeed recorded in the histories of Sonoma County. See Ernest L. Finley, *History of Sonoma County* (Santa Rosa: Press Democrat Publishing Co., 1937). According to local informants the half-house that was moved stood as a landmark for many years.

CAPTAIN JACK

The saga of Captain Jack and the Modoc War is both history and legend. No one knows for sure how he would have told his full story, but his final courtroom speech as recorded here was true. When he sat down a profound silence enveloped the courtroom for several moments. Yes, the war was over. Jack and three others paid with their lives. The rest were sent to prison or to a reservation. There are many versions of this war;

this is only one Indian's. But regardless of the point of view there is tragic irony in the story because this unfortunate affair could have been avoided. It cost the government almost as much as it cost to fight the Spanish-American war; a good reservation could have been purchased for much less, and countless lives could have been saved. Now there is a national monument at the lava beds where the story of Captain Jack can be told. And Captain Jack is only a bitter memory.

Much has been written about this historic incident and, like the story of General Custer's death, the facts blend with the legend according to the perceptions of the historian. Joaquin Miller in *Life Amongst the Modocs* felt a personal involvement with the Indians and his views were sentimental. Jeff Riddle, in *The Indian History of the Modoc War*, gives another contemporary version of the story. For more recent interpretations see Doris Palmer Payne's *Captain Jack, Modoc Renegade*, Keith A. Murray's *The Modocs and Their Wars*, and Richard Dillon's *Burnt-out Fires*.

DORSEY THE MAILMAN

The legend of Dorsey comes from the Henry W. Splitter Collection in the archives of the Folklore and Mythology Center, University of California, Los Angeles. This collection consists of clippings and excerpts from nineteenth century newspapers and books about the Old West.

Sources cited by Splitter are W.P. Bartlett, *Happenings: A Series of Sketches of the Great California Out-of-Doors* (Los Angeles, 1927); and WPA Writers' Project, *The Old West: Pioneer Tales of San Bernardino County* (San Bernardino, 1940). See also Cora L. Keagle, "Calico's Canine Carrier," *The Desert Magazine*, June, 1943. The story of Dorsey is told again in *Calico Ghost Town* (Ghost Town, California: Knott's Berry Farm, 1959).

Dorsey has now become immortal, along with other heroes of the movies. A Disney film was made of his career in Calico; it was called, "Go West, Young Dog." Not having seen it, we cannot vouch for its authenticity.

THE MYSTERY OF MURIETA'S HEAD

For the most recent study of this legendary character, see Frank F. Latta, *Joaquin Murrieta and His Horse Gangs* (Santa Cruz, 1980). Also see Joseph Henry Jackson, *Bad Company* (Lincoln, 1977), originally published in 1939 as *Tin-types in Gold*; Yellow Bird (pseud. John Rollin Ridge), *The Life and Adventures of Joaquin Murieta, the Celebrated California Bandit* (New edition, Norman, 1955). Other useful works are Walter

Noble Burns, *The Robin Hood of El Dorado: The Saga of Joaquin Murieta* (New York, 1932); John C. Cunningham, *The Truth about Murieta* (Los Angeles, 1938); Francis P. Farquhar, *Joaquin Murieta, The Brigand Chief of California* (San Francisco, 1932); William B. Secrest, *Joaquin, Bloody Bandit of the Mother Lode* (Fresno, 1967); and Raymond F. Wood, "New Light on Joaquin Murieta," *The Pacific Historian*, 14 (Winter, 1970), 54-65.

Recent tales related to Joaquin may be found in Hector Lee, *Tales of California* (Logan, Utah, 1974); *California Folklore Archive* (Chico, 1950); San Francisco *Chronicle*, April 30, 1980; and personal letters and reports to the author from Marjorie Wellman McLain, Linda Ford, and Jack McAllister. Greater detail on the survival of Joaquin's head may be found in the author's "Joaquin Murieta," *Quarterly of the National Association and Center for Outlaw and Lawmen History*, 5:4 (July, 1980).

The material for this story was adapted from Hector H. Lee, "The Reverberant Joaquin Murieta in California Legendry," *The Pacific Historian*, 25:3 (Fall, 1981), 38-47.

LA LLORONA

Stories about La Llorona, the grieving woman or spectral siren (motif E574), are well known in Mexican families throughout California, Arizona, and Texas. Numerous examples have been collected, and at least two versions of the plaintive ballad about her have been recorded. Even the Ballet Folklorico of Mexico has enacted the legend in song and dance. Some scholars believe that the Llorona legend in America developed from a transplant of an old European tale, "Die Weisse Frau," in which the "white lady" killed her children in the mistaken belief that they stood in the way of her remarriage, a narrative known in Europe prior to the Spanish Conquest of Mexico. Others argue that the tale originated in Mexico, either from ancient Aztec lore or from a presumably real event concerning an Indian woman who had a Spaniard lover during the Conquest. The events comprising the version of the legend told here occurred in 1956 in Riverside, California. The motifs and characters are adapted from material presented in a paper by Terrence L. Hansen to the California Folklore Society in 1956.

For further reading see Bacil F. Kirtley, "La Llorona and Related Themes," *Western Folklore*, XIX (July, 1960), 155-168; Betty Leddy, "La Llorona in Southern Arizona," *Western Folklore*, VII (July, 1948), 272-277; Betty Leddy, "La Llorona Again," *Western Folklore*, IX (October, 1950), 363-365; Robert Barakat, "Wailing Women in Folklore," *Journal of American Folklore*, Vol. 82 (July-September, 1969), 270-272; Elaine K.

Miller, *Mexican Folk Narrative From the Los Angeles Area* (Austin: University of Texas Press, 1973). A version of the song is to be found in Frances Toor, *A Treasure of Mexican Folklore*, (New York: Crown Publishers, 1974), p. 443.

THE GHOST SHIP OF THE DESERT

The best known legend about ghostly ships is that of the *Flying Dutchman*, which is usually seen in bad weather off the Cape of Good Hope. Unlike most stories about phantom ships, whose doom results from a curse or a compact with an evil spirit, this California story is motivated by misfortune; the enemy is the impersonal machinery of nature.

The material for this story (motif E535) comes primarily from old newspaper reports found in the Henry W. Splitter collection in the archives of the Folklore and Mythology Center at the University of California, Los Angeles. Articles cited are from the San Francisco *Bulletin*, November 2 and October 26, 1870; the Los Angeles *News*, August 30, 1870; the Sacramento *Union*, August 8 and October 6, 1870; the Monterey *Democrat*, December 12, 1870; and the San Francisco *Examiner*, November 17, 1889. The story is also told by W.A. Chalfant in his *Tales of the Pioneers* (Stanford, 1942). Harold O. Weight, in "He Saw the Lost Desert Ship," *Westways*, November, 1965, tells of a man interviewed in 1907 who claimed to have found the lost ship and asserted that it contained gem stones including rubies and emeralds. The geologic formation which gives impetus to this legend is described by Ronald L. Ives, "The 'Phantom Ship' of the Gulf of California," *Western Folklore*, XVIII, No. 4 (October, 1959) 327.

And what about the possibility of pearls? In 1585 Hernando de Sanotis, a Royal Accountant, and his partners were granted a license to fish and trade for pearls off the coast of Mexico. By 1592, however, he had not exercised this privilege, so the license was transferred to Sebastian Vizcaino. In 1596 Vizcaino was able to outfit three ships in Acapulco, and with his young son aboard he sailed out for pearls and to find sites for new settlements. He proceeded up the Gulf of California in search of pearl oyster beds, but heavy storms forced him to return to Acapulco. See Michael Mathes, "California's First Explorer: Sebastian Vizcaino," *The Pacific Historian*, Vol. 25, No. 3 (Fall, 1981), p. 9.

BLOODSTAIN

The motif of the ineradicable bloodstain (E422.1.11.5) is not uncommon in American ghostlore. In this tale several other popular narrative elements are also to be found: noises presumably caused by ghostly persons (E402), ghost haunts house (E281.0.3), ghost unbolts the door (E279.2), and the sensitivity of animals to the presence of spirits. When told orally this can become a "jump" tale, which is designed to startle the audience at an unexpected point.

The basic story as told by Tom Moungovin of Fort Bragg is in the folklore archive at Sonoma State University. It was often recounted by Tom and other members of his family, and is still remembered by old-timers in western Mendocino County.

THE LADY OF THE LAKE

Except for stories like those about the vanishing hitchhiker or the claw hand, which are widespread throughout America, and a few other such universal supernatural characters and motifs, most ghost stories are strictly local legends. They are tied to a particular time and place, like haunted houses, and are told by or known to a limited group—a certain community, a professional or occupational circle, or a particular age group. But all such legends, whether local or widespread, borrow freely from popular motifs and conventional apparatus which are the common property of ghostlore everywhere. (motifs E275 and E334)

So our lady of the lake in this instance is a local legend. This version is adapted from Hector Lee, "Ghosts and Haunted Places," in the television series *There Is a Telling*, Vol. III, No. 4, KHSL-TV, Chico, California. The material was provided by James Payne and other informants in Alturas, California, for the folklore archives of Chico State College.

When told to an audience it is usually successful, if the timing is right, as a "jump" tale. That is, at its climax the audience can be startled by a loud noise or a sudden gesture. Mark Twain's famous "Golden Arm" story is a good example of this technique. But this story also gains credibility by having its roots in the historical wagon train migration to California in the 1850s.

THE BLUE LAKE MONSTER

Fabulous creatures in American folklore may be grouped in two categories: those which are generated by tall-tale artists for the sake of humor in exaggeration, and those which are believed to be real by those who attest to some actual visual contact with them. In the former group we find such unbelievables as the side-hill cougar, the hoop-snake, the hodag, the squonk, the gillygaloo (a side-hill plover which lays square eggs so they will not roll down steep inclines), the jack-a-lope (a cross between a jack rabbit and an antelope), the filla-ma-loo bird (which flies backwards), the wampus cat, the snipe, and other such whimsical whoppers. For a description of these uncanny creatures, with additional references, see Robert B. Downs, "Apocryphal Biology," in Mody C. Boatright, Robert B. Downs, and John T. Flanagan, *The Family Saga* (Urbana: University of Illinois Press, 1958), 20-48.

In the second group we must always consider the possibility that they really do exist. Documentation by people who claim to have seen UFOs cannot be dismissed lightly, and just as sincere are the many alleged witnesses to the existence of the Loch Ness Monster, Big Foot, the Abominable Snow Man, or the Bear Lake Monster in northern Utah.

The presence of a monster in the Blue Lakes of California was news in the 1870s, but the story seems to have died a natural death. Blue Lake is now a very popular fishing, boating, and recreation area. Reports that the Indians were superstitious of the place were probably greatly exaggerated. The older folk of the region, like Lake County's Historian Henry Mauldin remember the legend, but the newcomers have not exploited its advertising possibilities.

The material for the story we tell here, however, is documented. It comes from articles published in the *Russian River Flag*, a Healdsburg newspaper, on November 8, 1870, January 19, 1871, and May 11, 1871.

THE BUCKING BEAR OF BODEGA

Tellers of western tall tales are familiar with the motif of a man riding an unusual animal (X1004). One favorite yarn is about the man who mistakenly rode a wild bear thinking it was a tame one he had broken to the saddle. A good version is given by B.A. Botkin, *A Treasury of Western Folklore* (New York: Crown, 1951), p. 662. But such accounts are obvious lies. The Bodega story, on the other hand, has a certain flavor of credibility; it could have happened this way. But that is a matter for the reader to decide.

CHARLIE HANES

Although Charlie Hanes liked to let people believe that he made up this tale, and perhaps he thought so himself, it is really a very old one annotated as Tale Type 1881: "The Man Carried Through the Air by Geese," from the Baron Munchhausen tales. The motif of falling into a hollow stump with bear cubs (X1133.1) and getting out of the tree stump by grabbing the bear's tail (X1133.3) are listed by Baughman.

In his *America in Folklore* (Chicago: University of Chicago Press, 1959), Richard Dorson tells the story of how Davy Crockett escaped from a hollow tree: "He tumbled into the hollow and landed in a pile of swallows' dung. Davy groped around in the darkness and felt the fur of a hibernating bear. He seized the bear's tail with his teeth, prodded his rump with his butcher knife, and so ascended the steep hole by bear power. Although realistically set on the Tennessee frontier, this yarn closely follows a European folktale, 'How the Man Came out of the Tree Stump,' pulled by the bear's tail."

BIG FOOT

The Jenkins story of Big Foot which is retold here was collected and recorded on tape March 12, 1963, by Ronald Washburn for the Sonoma State University folklore archive. Other versions of similar sightings are frequently reported by the press, radio, and television, and there are many people who sincerely believe that the legend is true.

Similar humanoid monsters have been reported in other parts of the country, too. Thus the legend grows. Like the fabulous Loch Ness Monster or the Abominable Snowman, Big Foot has yet to be proved real. Until then, he or she will remain a mystery and a creature of folklore. Notes about Big Foot are to be found in *Western Folklore*, October, 1964, p. 271; and April, 1965, p. 119.